THE 1483 GLOUCESTER
CHARTER IN HISTORY

THE 1483 GLOUCESTER CHARTER IN HISTORY

N.M. HERBERT
R.A. GRIFFITHS
SUSAN REYNOLDS
PETER CLARK

Published for
The Gloucester City Council
and
The Gloucester Civic Trust

by
ALAN SUTTON
1983

Alan Sutton Publishing Limited
17a Brunswick Road
Gloucester GL1 1HG

First published 1983

Cover design based on posters by Philip Moss

ISBN 0 86299 061 0

Typesetting and origination by
Alan Sutton Publishing Limited
Photoset Palatino 10/12
Printed in Great Britain

TABLE OF CONTENTS

Foreword   7

Charter of Richard III to Gloucester, Granted by Letters Patent   9
2 September 1483
Newly translated by Dr N.M. Herbert

I   1483: Gloucester's Livelihood in the Middle Ages   16
Dr N.M. Herbert, Editor of the Gloucestershire
Victoria County History

II   Richard III: King or Anti-King?   29
Professor R.A. Griffiths,
University College, Swansea

III   1483: Gloucester and Town Government in the Middle Ages   40
Miss Susan Reynolds, Fellow and Tutor,
Lady Margaret Hall, Oxford

IV   A Poisoned Chalice? The 1483 Charter, City and County
1483–1662   52
Mr Peter Clark, Reader in Social History,
University of Leicester

FOREWORD

The lectures that follow were arranged to take place in the early part of 1983 in order to provide some historical background to the celebration of 'Gloucester 500' in the late summer. They were a co-operative venture, organized by the Gloucester City Council and the Gloucester Civic Trust in conjuction with the Cheltenham and Gloucester branch of the Historical Association, the Gloucester and District Archaeological Research Group, and the Bristol and Gloucestershire Archaeological Society.

A large number of people were involved in the whole venture, but it is right to make special mention both of our four lecturers and of Mrs. Evelyn Christmas, who was responsible for all the correspondence and for many of the practical arrangements. I must myself take responsibility for any editorial errors that remain in the published version of the lectures.

June 1983
DAVID M. PATON

THE CHARTER OF RICHARD III TO GLOUCESTER, GRANTED BY LETTERS PATENT 2 SEPTEMBER 1483

Richard, by the grace of God King of England and France and lord of Ireland, to all to whom the present letters come, greetings. We have inspected letters patent of our brother, the lord Edward IV, late King of England, made in these words ... (there then follows a recital, occupying the first half of the charter, of the letters patent of Edward IV dated 1462 and inspecting and confirming letters patent of Henry VI, 1423: inspecting and confirming a charter of Henry V, 1415: inspecting and confirming a charter of Henry IV, 1399: inspecting and confirming a charter of Richard II, 1398: granting additional liberties and inspecting and confirming his own letters patent, 1378: inspecting and confirming a charter of Edward III, 1328: inspecting and confirming a charter of Edward II, 1312: granting an additional liberty and inspecting, confirming and reciting two charters of Henry II, a charter of Richard I granted in 1194, a charter of King John granted in 1200, and charters of Henry III granted in 1227 and 1256).

We now moreover, of our especial grace, by the wording of these presents ratify and confirm to the said burgesses, their heirs, and successors the said gifts, grants, confirmations, liberties, privileges, franchises, acquittances, immunities, articles and customs and everything else contained and specified in the said charters and letters, as the said charters and letters bear witness in due form. Furthermore we wish to show the said burgesses fuller favour in this regard.

We have granted to the said burgesses, their heirs, and successors, and by this charter have confirmed for us and our heirs and successors, that they may fully enjoy and use forever, without let or hindrance from us or our heirs or our justiciars, escheators, sheriffs, coroners, or other bailiffs or ministers whatever, any of the gifts, grants, confirmations, orders, liberties, privileges, franchises, acquittances, immunities, articles, or customs or anything else contained in the said charters or letters that have not been used up to the present time.

9

Furthermore, because of the special affection which we bear towards the said town of Gloucester and its bailiffs and burgesses, and considering the good and faithful actions of the said bailiffs and burgesses in causes of particular importance to us, and wishing to provide for their immunity, protection and peace, we, of our special favour and from certain knowledge and free impulse, have remitted and released for us, our heirs and successors, to the burgesses, their heirs and successors, £45, parcel of the £65 owed for the farm of the town or borough of Gloucester.

Furthermore of our fuller favour we grant to the said burgesses that on the Monday after the feast of St.Michael the Archangel next they may choose from among themselves a suitable mayor, who is to make an oath in the presence of the bailiffs and four of the more law-abiding and prudent burgesses of the town that he will perform the duties that pertain to the office of mayor in the said town.

Furthermore of our fuller favour we grant to the burgesses that, by whatever name or names they are styled in the grants made to them or their ancestors or predecessors by our forefathers or predecessors, from now on the mayor and burgesses are one corporate body by the name of 'the mayor and burgesses of the town of Gloucester' and by that name are able in person and capable in law of acquiring lands and tenements, to hold to them and their successors in fee and perpetuity and by whatever form of tenure from whatever persons or person who wish to grant the same to them; and they may hold all lands, tenements, possessions and hereditaments which the said burgesses or their predecessors have held at any time; and they and their successors by name of the mayor and burgesses of the town of Gloucester may plead and be impleaded, make answer or cause to answer, in any kind of actions, real or personal, before us and our heirs in Chancery, before our justices of King's Bench, Barons of the Exchequer, the steward and marshal of our household or before any other justices in any kind of court in the realm of England.

Also, we grant that the mayor and his successors in the office shall have a sword carried before him within the town and its liberties, in the same manner as is the custom in other cities and towns in the realm of England.

Wishing moreover to show greater favour to the said mayor and burgesses, we grant them by these presents that they may elect from among themselves 12 aldermen who will perform in the town of Gloucester all the duties that the aldermen of our city of London perform. And we wish and grant that the said 12 aldermen, thus

10

elected, will take their oath before the mayor of the town of Gloucester in the same manner as the aldermen of our city of London do upon their election, And we wish and grant that whenever any alderman, thus elected, shall die in office that then the surviving aldermen shall come together without delay to choose in his place a new alderman from among the more law-abiding and prudent burgesses of the town; this is to be done whenever necessary and without obtaining any licence from us, our heirs and successors. The said alderman, thus elected, is to take his oath as aforesaid and perform everything as the aldermen of the city of London do.

Furthermore, of our abundant grace, we wish and grant by these presents to the said burgesses that the said town of Gloucester together with all the townships and hamlets in the hundreds of Dudstone and King's Barton next Gloucester, which are within the county of Gloucestershire, shall from the said Monday after Michaelmas next be incorporated in fact and in name as one entire county, entirely distinct and separate from and no parcel of the county of Gloucestershire, and shall be known forever by the name of 'the county of the town of Gloucester'; saving and reserving to us and our heirs, however, that the various justices assigned to hold the assizes, deliver the gaol, and keep the peace within the county of Gloucestershire and our sheriff of Gloucestershire in holding his shire courts may be free, and may have free access to the town for holding the said sessions and shires for all matters arising outside the said county of the town of Gloucester and within the county of Gloucestershire, as they have been accustomed to hold them, the present grant notwithstanding.

We wish also that the bailiffs of the town henceforth to be chosen shall be chosen in the same place, time, and manner as they were in the time of our brother, the lord Edward IV, late King of England, or as they have ever been accustomed to be chosen. And that if any bailiff of the town, after being elected into the office, shall die within one year of his election then the burgesses of the town of Gloucester shall without delay choose another in his place from among the more law-abiding and prudent burgesses of the town; they may do this whenever necessary and without obtaining any licence from us, our heirs and successors. The said bailiff, thus elected, having taken his oath in the customary manner, shall have such power, authority and jurisdiction in all matters as the bailiffs of that town have ever had.

Also we wish and grant them by these presents that the bailiffs of the town who are in office on the said Monday, and the bailiffs who are chosen in the future, shall from the said Monday be the sheriffs of the said county of the town of Gloucester. And that both those who hold the office of sheriffs of the county of the town of Gloucester and the office of bailiffs there shall exercise all the liberties, franchises, and customs formerly used there according to the form and effect of the franchises, liberties and customs used by virtue of the grants of divers of our forefathers and ancestors and all customs used there up to the present time, the present grant notwithstanding. Those who are sheriffs of the county of the town of Gloucester on the said Monday and all others who are sheriffs in future shall, after their election, in the customary manner before the mayor of the town of Gloucester (and not before anyone else) in the gildhall of the said town (and not elsewhere) take oath to perform faithfully while in office everything that belongs to the office of sheriff. The mayor of the town of Gloucester will from time to time without delay certify into Chancery, by his letters patent sealed with the seal of office of the mayoralty of the town, the names of the sheriffs of the county of the town. The sheriffs of the county of the town of Gloucester are to hold from month to month on Tuesdays in the said town our shire courts for the said town and hundreds; and they will have and exercise all the powers, jurisdiction, authority and liberty and whatever else belongs to the office of sheriff in the town and hundreds and whatever else our sheriffs in our realm of England have or ought to have in their bailiwicks.

And from the said Monday we and our heirs and successors will direct all writs, precepts, orders and commands concerning matters arising within the town of Gloucester and the hundreds and precincts — and which, if the town, hundreds and precincts had not been made into a separate county, would have been directed to the sheriff of the county of Gloucestershire and served and executed by him — to the sheriffs of the county of the town of Gloucester. And from the said Monday no other sheriff of our realm of England or any sheriff's bailiff or serjeant, apart from our sheriffs of the county of the town of Gloucester and their bailiffs and ministers, shall enter the said town, hundreds and precincts to perform anything that belongs to the office of sheriff nor in any way intermeddle in the same, with the exception of our sheriff of the county of Gloucestershire holding the shire courts as aforesaid. And each sheriff of the county of the town of Gloucester and bailiff of the town who holds the office after the said Monday must render his account each year before our Treasurer and Barons of the Exchequer, or before the Barons alone, for the issues which belong or should belong to his office. He may do all that concerns his office through sufficient attorneys, appointed by his letters patent, addressed to the said Barons; no sheriff of the county of the town of Gloucester or bailiff of the town is to be compelled to come outside the county in person to account for anything connected with his office if he prefers to appoint attornies to do it for him.

Wishing furthermore to show our fuller favour to the said mayor and burgesses of the town of Gloucester and their successors we have granted, and grant by these presents, that they may choose from among themselves and have in the said town for ever, a coroner, who is to be elected and removed from office at the will and pleasure of the said mayor and aldermen and who is to perform everything that belongs to the office of coroner in the said town, hundreds and precincts; as soon as he is elected the coroner is to take his oath before the mayor and sheriffs in the customary manner that he will perform all the duties that belong to the office. Whenever a coroner, elected as aforesaid, should die or be removed from office by the mayor and aldermen we wish and grant that the mayor and burgesses elect another coroner in his place without delay; they may do this whenever necessary and without obtaining any licence from us, our heirs and successors. The said coroner, having been elected and taken his oath, shall perform everything that belongs to the office.

Also we wish and grant by these presents to the said burgesses and their successors that, after they by virtue of this grant have once chosen a mayor, who has made his oath as aforesaid, then continually in the future a mayor will be chosen each year on the said Monday by the 12 aldermen and 12 of the more law-abiding and prudent burgesses of the town. If any mayor after being elected to office should die within a year following his election the 12 aldermen and 12 burgesses may without delay choose another mayor in his place from among themselves; they may do this whenever it is necessary and without obtaining any licence from us, our heirs and successors. The said mayor, thus elected, will take his oath of office before the coroner of the town of Gloucester in the presence of 6 aldermen; and no mayor of the town at any future time shall be compelled to take his oath of office before the Barons of the Exchequer or anywhere else than in the said town.

Also we wish and grant that there shall be each year in the said town of Gloucester 4 serjeants-at-mace, two of them assigned to serve the mayor and the other two to serve the sheriffs of the county of the town.

And furthermore of our fuller favour we grant by these presents that the mayor of the town and his successors shall in future, both in our presence and our absence, hold and exercise within the town, hundreds and precincts the office of the clerk of the market of our household, together with everything that belongs to the office in all matters concerning it there, and with all the profits, fines, amercements, and compositions arising from the office which should be levied and taken for use of the mayor, without rendering any account to us. And in future no clerk of the market of our household apart from the said mayor of the town may have access to the town, hundreds or precincts to perform anything that belongs to the office or by colour of his office intermeddle in any way in the town.

Furthermore we have granted and by these presents grant that the mayors of the town may in future, without hindrance from us or our heirs, perform everything that belongs or should belong to the office of steward and marshal of our household in the town as freely, quietly and as fully as any steward and marshal of our household. And that no mayor, sheriff, bailiff nor any inhabitant of the town, hundreds and precincts shall be required to accept or execute any order made by a steward or marshal of our household or his proxy or deputy, nor appear before them in any cause, nor be obedient to their mandates. And no steward or marshal of our household, nor any deputy or minister of his court, apart from the said mayor and his ministers, may, in our presence or absence, have access to the town, hundreds or precincts to hold any session or inquisition or any pleas, nor to execute any writ, nor to perform anything concerned with their offices or arising from any other matter.

Furthermore we have granted and by these presents grant that the mayor and alderman of the town, duly elected and appointed, shall have forever full powers to enquire into, hear and determine all matters, pleas, defaults, causes and articles which belong to the office of justices of the peace, labourers and artificers, and all matters arising within the town, hundreds and precincts which ought to be enquired into the determined by the said justices; and they are to exercise those powers as fully and completely as the justices of the peace, labourers and artificers and the justices for hearing and determining felonies, trespasses and misdemeanours within the county of Gloucestershire have done up to now, without any of the said justices in the county of Gloucestershire or any sheriff or bailiff of the town of Gloucester intermeddling in any cause, pleas, defaults, or articles or anything arising from any cause that belongs to the jurisdiction of those justices in the town, hundreds and precincts.

Moreover we wish and grant to the mayor and burgesses that the mayor of the town of Gloucester and his successors, duly elected and sworn in before the coroner of the town as aforesaid, may be our

escheator in the county of the town of Gloucester and perform everything that belongs to the office of escheator in the said county; and that
no other escheator of our realm of England apart from the said mayor
may for any cause whatever have access to the county of the town of
Gloucester to perform anything that belongs to the office of escheator.
Every mayor of the town who holds office after the said Monday shall
account each year before the Barons of the Exchequer for all the profits
belonging to the office of escheator of the county of the town and may
have the right to appoint by his letters patent directed to the said Barons
sufficient attornies to account for him. And no mayor of the town is to be
compelled to come outside the town to account in person for anything
belonging to the office of escheator or to do anything else in his capacity
as mayor or escheator if he prefers to appoint an attorney to do it for
him.

Moreover we wish and grant that the said mayor and burgesses and
their successors may, clause by clause, hold and use all other franchises,
liberties, privileges, immunities, quittances and customs which the said
bailiffs and burgesses and their ancestors and predecessors have held
and used before this present grant by grant of our ancestors or by right
of custom, the present grant and all contained in it notwithstanding.
And they shall pay no fine or fee to us, or our heirs and successors for
any of the foregoing, for which reason there shall be no express mention
by us in the present grant of the true annual value of the foregoing or of
the other grants made to the said burgesses by us or our ancestors, no
other statute, act, ordinance, restriction or order or other matter
withstanding.

We wish also that, whereas the burgesses and inhabitants of the town
of Tewkesbury and their ancestors and predecessors have from time
immemorial been quit by land and sea of toll, custom, pavage, murage,
pontage, passage, keyage, lastage, pickage, stickage, stallage, pannage
and all other customs in Gloucester and its liberty, they may continue to
be quit of the said dues forever and without contradiction, notwithstanding anything to the contrary in any grants of us, our ancestors or
predecessors, to the burgesses of the town of Gloucester.

In witness whereof we have made these letters patent, witnessed by
me at Westminster, 2 September in the first year of our reign.

(By writ of the Privy Seal dated as above)

15

I

GLOUCESTER'S LIVELIHOOD IN THE LATE MIDDLE AGES

By 1483, when Gloucester's progress towards full civic liberties culmin-
ated in the charter of incorporation, its greatest days were in the most
obvious sense long past. In the two and a half centuries after the
Norman Conquest the town's vital strategic position, commanding the
lowest bridge over the Severn, had made it a place where kings felt it
advisable periodically to establish their court and government, where
armies were mustered and equipped against the Welsh, and where
dissident barons in times of internal strife sought to secure a military
base. In the late Middle Ages, however, such excitements were rare. The
parliament of 1378, held in St, Peter's Abbey, was a late renewal of the
town's role as a temporary seat of government; the closure of the Severn
crossing to Queen Margaret's army before the battle of Tewkesbury in
1471 was an isolated involvement in military affairs. For the most part
Gloucester was left in peace to perform those more mundane economic
and social functions which had provided its livelihood even when it was
a frequent participant in great events on the national stage.
   The more important of those functions were performed in a local
region which covered the northern two-thirds of Gloucestershire and
some adjoining parts of Herefordshire and Worcestershire. To that
region, in which no major rival to its hegemony had arisen from all the
places that acquired urban characteristics in the centuries following the
Conquest, it supplied imported goods, brought up river from Bristol or
overland from London, and manufactured goods, produced by its own
iron, cloth and leather industries. It also marketed agricultural produce
for a much smaller area of Vale and Severnside villages, and it was the
seat of the county administration. Its geographical position, however,
enabled it also to play a part in the movement of goods and people from
outside its region. Its position at the Severn crossing and on another
important land route — that down the Vale of Gloucester — meant that

16

trade into and out of South Wales and between the Midlands and Bristol would always be significant for its livelihood. The navigable river brought it at least the potential for a major share in river trade and for a role as a port for export trade. This account will examine the evidence for Gloucester's performance of those varied functions between the late 14th century and the early 16th and will attempt, in the face of a sad lack of local documentation, to make a general assessment of its economic fortunes at the period.

During most of the Middle Ages Gloucester had a small group of men who gained a living from *overseas trade* with the Continent and with Ireland. At the beginning of our period, in the late 14th century and the early 15th, four or five fairly wealthy merchants are recorded, most notably John Banbury (d. *c.*1404) who made large investments in property in the town. References to merchants in Gloucester are sparse in the middle and later years of the 15th century, but another three or four were trading there in the early years of the 16th, including David Vaughan who was mentioned in 1502 as importing goods in a 100-ton vessel, built to his own order. The cargoes imported by such Gloucester merchants included wine, salt fish and Baltic timber, while they sent down river, for export, cloth and corn. Corn was recorded as an important element in Gloucester's down-river trade from the mid 14th century and the trade evidently continued in the early 16th when much of the corn brought in from the surrounding countryside was carted directly to the town quay and sold there. There appears to be a total lack of evidence for the corn trade in the middle and later 15th century, though it would be unwise to assume just from that a loss or severe decline in the trade. One fact that could suggest such a decline, however, was the Crown's response to Gloucester's request for measures to help its economy in 1447 — permission to build two corn-mills at Westgate Bridge; the new mills may have been part of efforts being made to revive the grain trade on the river.

Although it had some merchants at the period, Gloucester was not then — or at any time before the opening of the Gloucester and Berkeley Canal in 1827 — a port of any significance for overseas trade. Before that date the narrows and shallows of the difficult stretch of river below the town posed too many problems for seagoing vessels. In medieval times when such vessels were still very small more of them perhaps did come up to the quay than in later centuries, but the available evidence suggests that for its overseas trade the town was mainly dependent on Bristol. The evidence for this, as for much about medieval Gloucester, is sparse but it seems more than chance that most of the references that have survived to Gloucester men importing goods show them acting through Bristol, where the cargoes would be transhipped into river craft. Some use was probably made also of the 'creeks' of the Severn estuary below Gloucester, such as Frampton on Severn, Newnham and the tiny hamlet of Gatcombe, in Awre parish. Gatcombe, in particular, was well established as an outlet for Gloucester's overseas trade by the 1580s and, though the only possible evidence for the connexion at an earlier date was the Gatcombe man mentioned as owning property in the town before 1509, it had probably long been used as such. Some merchants, whether from Gloucester or elsewhere, were certainly using Gatcombe by 1354 when it was recorded that they would come to make offerings at a statue of the Virgin Mary in the porch of Awre church before going overseas.

With few seagoing vessels penetrating so far up the Severn, the most use made of Gloucester quay was by the Severn trows and other river craft, maintaining the connexion with Bristol and also carrying on *trade within the river* . Among cargoes shipped to Gloucester were wood and coal from places up river in Worcestershire and Staffordshire, market produce from some of the riverside villages nearer at hand, and stone (the grey lias limestone quarried on Severnside), loaded at places like Elmore and Minsterworth. The conclusion to be reached, however, is that even as a port for the internal river trade Gloucester did not realize its potential. In the late-medieval records very few occupations concerned with the river trade occur; a roll of non-freeman inhabitants in 1423 lists only a single trowman and only three boatmen appear among all entrants to the freedom of the town in the ten years from 1535 to 1545. This seems to reflect the fact that much of Gloucester's trade with other places on the river, and possibly with Bristol also, was in the hands of outsiders, particularly the monopolistic trow-owners of the town of Bewdley, in Worcestershire. As early as 1411 the Gloucester burgesses, together with those of Bristol, complained that they were being forced to hire Bewdley trows at extortionate prices for carrying their goods on the upper part of the river; some Gloucester men, attempting to bring wood past Bewdley on some kind of raft, had been attacked and their cargo lost. Seventy years later, in 1481, seven Bewdley boats were recorded as trading regularly to Gloucester quay. From nearer at hand, the town of Tewkesbury was also a rival to Gloucester in the river trade, particularly for that important down-river trade in corn. That rivalry was probably only one of several matters that caused tension between the two towns. A tailpiece to the 1483 charter, confirming Tewkesbury men as free of tolls in Gloucester, probably reflects long years of bickering over trading matters.

Gloucester's failure to get a significant share in the river trade, the fact that much of that trade was carried on between Bristol and places up river and bypassed Gloucester, and its dependence on Bristol for its overseas trade were all causes of resentment to Gloucester men. That resentment no doubt played a part in those attempts to wrest some profit from the passing trade on the river which are a recurrent feature of Gloucester's history over several centuries. Complaints that the Gloucester bailiffs were stopping or illegally levying tolls on boats carrying goods between Bristol and the up-river towns were recorded from 1400 and resulted in a Star Chamber suit in 1505 after an Act of Parliament had declared the Severn to be a toll-free river. In the latter suit Gloucester and Worcester registered claims to levy tolls on cargoes landed at their quays or merely passing under their bridges and were opposed by the trowmen of Tewkesbury, Bewdley and other places on the river. The trowmen complained that the Gloucester burgesses shot arrows or threw stones at their boats in order to force them into the bank and sometimes made them sell their goods in the town.

Examination of the evidence for the main currents of internal *long-distance trade* that flowed into and through Gloucester reveals once more the magnetic pull exerted by the great seaport of Bristol. Trade routes to Bristol from the Welsh Marches, from much of the Midlands and from places further north came through Gloucester. Some of the merchants from that vast hinterland traded goods in the town as they passed to and fro, while a greater number no doubt used it as a staging-post and took advantage of its facilities for road transport. Mentioned in the records of the period are traders from such towns as Ludlow (who probably used river transport, shipping their goods at Bewdley) and Leominster, and from as far away as Chester and Manchester; particularly regular visitors seem to have been merchants from the great Midland trading town of Coventry, a place which looked to Bristol as its main export outlet. Gloucester could never rival Bristol as a port for overseas trade, but it was at least in a position geographically to gain some advantage from Bristol's far-flung trading links.

A connexion with another great port maintained at the period was that with Southampton, from which were carried woad and madder, the dyestuffs used in the cloth-making industry, together with wine. In the 1430s and the 1440s a merchant called Philip Monger controlled the Gloucester end of that trade and seems to have prospered by it, for he and his wife paid for the rebuilding of the chapel of St. Thomas outside the north gate. Gloucester tradesmen also had regular connexions with London mercers and other wholesalers and already by 1381 there seems to have been a service operated by carrier's wagon between Gloucester and the capital. Another regular trade from much nearer at hand was represented by the Droitwich salters who were listed among visiting traders in the 1390s and 1481.

One direction in which the influence of Gloucester as a trading centre was particularly evident at the period was into South Wales. Indications of the importance of that trade in the 15th century include the six men from the town of Brecon who were paying the bailiffs for the right of trading in Gloucester in 1423, while from further along the same route the town of Llandovery sent six traders, three of them dealers in cloth, in 1481. Probably also continuing throughout the late Middle Ages was the cattle trade out of Wales, which had been established by the mid 13th century. Its Welsh trade was one of the most stable elements in Gloucester's economic history, and the causeway and bridges over the Severn, by which, as the burgesses said in 1505, 'all the king's subjects have their passage between England and Wales with their goods and chattels and all other merchandise', were prized as among the town's most valuable assets. Gifts of money for their upkeep figured frequently in the wills of burgesses of the 15th century and the early 16th, and more substantial endowments were provided by leading inhabitants, including two former mayors John Caple and Thomas Bell.

For making an assessment of the more *local trade* conducted by Gloucester in the late Middle Ages fuller evidence is available. For five years (those beginning at Michaelmas 1380, 1396, 1398, 1423 and 1481) there survive the rolls on which each year the bailiffs entered the names of unfranchised traders, who paid an annual composition for the right of trading in the town or for exercising a craft there; they included not only those inhabitants of the town who had not acquired trading rights as freemen but also a large number of 'foreign' traders, most of them identified by their town or village of origin. The lists reveal that, as one would expect, the trade in basic market produce was confined to a relatively small surrounding area of the Vale and Severnside. The villages from which men came regularly to Gloucester market mostly lay within or close to an often-quoted limit of 6⅔ miles given by Bracton, the 13th-century jurist, for the usual day's market journey, including at the outer limits such places as Tirley, Great Witcombe, Standish, and Huntley. Beyond that limit a ring of smaller market towns restricted Gloucester's role as a market for agricultural produce; it had little impact, for example, above the Cotswold ridge where Painswick and

Cirencester provided market centres for such local produce. A few villages from well beyond the basic Gloucester market area do figure on the rolls, their presence — as in the case of some Stroud Valley villages mentioned below — probably explained by a trade in some particular commodity.

Most of the more distant places which appear on the rolls of traders were other market towns, illustrating Gloucester's important function as a distributor of goods to the lesser towns of the region. A ring of market towns within about 20 miles of Gloucester, including Northleach, Cirencester, Tetbury, Berkeley, Lydney, Ross-on-Wye, and Ledbury were represented. Most of those places sent one or two traders each year, the notable exception being Ross which sent as many as eight in 1423; significantly it stood on Gloucester's main trade route into Wales. The two nearest market towns, Painswick and Newent, at six and eight miles respectively, each sent between 5 and 9 traders in the last years of the 14th century and were evidently very much satellites of Gloucester for trade purposes.

The rolls also provide some indications of the commodities that bulked largest in Gloucester's local trade at the period. There are, not surprisingly, references to the trade in fish, a significant one for Gloucester throughout the Middle Ages. Salmon and lamprey were brought from Severnside villages and hamlets such as Longney and Epney, in Moreton Valence, as well as from two of the market towns, Ross and Chepstow, and traders from other towns — Cheltenham, Evesham, and Winchcombe — were also recorded as dealing in fish. This suggests that Gloucester was acting as a centre for distributing the products of the Severn and Wye fisheries to towns further inland, and also figuring in that trade were no doubt the herring and other saltwater fish that were imported to the area from Ireland in large quantities at the period. Wool, sold in the official wool-market in the Boothall in Westgate Street and at the annual fairs, was another important commodity, particularly for the supply of the town's cloth-making and capping industries. Wool-merchants from such Cotswold places as Cirencester and Tormarton are mentioned in the records, and wool was also brought from places further afield, including Coventry and North Wiltshire. A commodity particularly vital to another of the town's industries figures on the roll of traders for 1380, which records 6 men carrying in iron on packhorses; no places of origin are given for them but all came in by the west gate and so were presumably from the Forest of Dean. The needs of another of Gloucester's industries, tanning, would have dictated that other items of incoming trade were oak-bark and hides. Packs of ready-tanned leather also came in from some of the market towns.

For the most part the available sources provide only clues to the type of goods that were brought in to the town. It can be assumed, however, that the traders from Gloucester's region returned to their towns and villages with the fabrics, wines, spices and dyestuffs that the Gloucester merchants and wholesalers had obtained from London, Bristol and Southampton, as well as with the iron goods, cloth and leather goods produced by the town's own manufacturing industries. The importance of this function of supplying the lesser towns of its region is underlined by the fact that when, at the end of the period, a clear picture emerges of the dominant class in the town it was provided chiefly by men from the distributive trades who sustained this function. The records reveal the occupations of 43 (just over half the total) of all the men who held office as mayor or sheriff in the years 1483 to 1546; they were 10 drapers, 8 mercers, 5 merchants, 4 cappers, 3 tanners, 2 clothiers, 2 lawyers, 2 brewers, a goldsmith, a vintner, a dyer, a bellfounder, a cutler, a wire-drawer, and a butcher.

In an examination of the evidence for Gloucester's *industry* in the late Middle Ages, the first consideration must be to see how its traditional trades of metal-working and cloth-making fared. In the 12th and 13th centuries the town had been known throughout England for its iron goods. The industry was stimulated then by the military and naval requirements of the Crown and in particular was well placed to make a contribution to campaigns in Wales and Ireland. In 1228, for example, Henry III at Kerry, in Montgomeryshire, and in need of axes, mattocks and rock-cutting tools, turned naturally to the Gloucester smiths. Another order of the same king, in 1242, shows that the industry then had the capacity and organization to produce 10,000 horseshoes and 100,000 nails and deliver them to Portsmouth within 20 days. By the 15th century the industry had lost this military significance and it would seem that its greatest days were past. Nevertheless it still retained considerable strength and variety: in the records of the late 14th century and the 15th 17 different metal-working trades were mentioned. Of particular importance was the making of cutlery: there were 8 cutlers among the non-freeman inhabitants alone in 1423 and 12 were mentioned as householders in the 1455 rental of the town. The making of pins, in later centuries to become Gloucester's most important trade, was recorded in the town from 1396 and was well established by the first decade of the 16th century when 6 pinners and 2 wiredrawers were mentioned in the hundred court records. Gloucester's famous trade of bell-founding probably also continued throughout the period, but there appears to be a gap in the definite evidence between Henry Prince, mentioned as a founder in 1398, and the prosperous William Henshaw who served the first of five terms as mayor in 1503. Other specialist craftsmen at the period included blade-smiths, spurriers, lorimers, locksmiths and nailers, and metal-working in general seems to have been the industry that the townspeople themselves still regarded as their most significant. Horseshoes and nails were depicted on the seal of office struck for the mayor after the granting of the 1483 charter, and the same devices were used again on the coat-of-arms awarded to the town in 1538.

An industry with almost as long a recorded history as metal-working in Gloucester was cloth-making. The movement of the cloth industry from the towns out into country districts has in the past been seen as an important factor in the decline of towns in the late Middle Ages. Gloucester did not lose its cloth industry at the period: weavers remained a numerous group of craftsmen in the town and in the 1530s were the largest group seeking admission as freemen, and the other trades of the industry — dyers, fullers and shearmen — were still in evidence. It may be, however, that already by the beginning of our period the finishing processes of the industry had begun to move out to the Stroud valleys, where fulling-mills were established by the middle of the 14th century. On the rolls of traders mentioned above villagers who came from beyond the town's basic market area included some from the Stroud area and among them in the 1390s were a fuller from Woodchester and a dyer from King's Stanley and, in 1481, a fuller from Stroud. It is possible that those men were contracted to do finishing work for Gloucester masters. There were certainly connexions of this kind by the early 16th century. The clothier John Sandford, who worked a fulling-mill at Stonehouse, was settled in Gloucester as a leading burgess in the 1540s, and it was perhaps more than just as an investment that the wealthy Gloucester mercer John Cooke bought a fulling-mill at Ebley, near Stroud, in 1524.

If a change of that kind had led to some loss of employment, it was compensated at the end of the period by the rise of a new textile trade, the making of woollen caps. That trade was established in the town by 1481 and at least nine cappers were in business there in the years 1502–7. In the next generation the trade was to produce two particularly notable mayors of the town, Thomas Bell and John Falconer, whose time was looked back on in the late 16th century as something of a 'golden age' for industry in Gloucester. Bell alone was said to employ over 300 people in

1538 and his success in business enabled him to buy up much of the property that came on the market by the dissolution of the town's religious houses and chantries.

The third main strand in the town's traditional pattern of industry was provided by the leather trades and they, too, maintained their importance at the period. Tanners remained a wealthy and fairly prominent group, and, among humbler leather-workers, cordwainers were particularly numerous. The tanners and cordwainers were among the earliest trades to form themselves into trade companies when such organizations start to appear in Gloucester in the later 15th century. The town also had the usual variety of service trades, such as building workers and the suppliers of food and drink. Overall, therefore, it can be shown that, though important changes were taking place in the nature of its two principal industries of metal-working and woollens, Gloucester retained a substantial industrial base at the period.

Gloucester's functions as a town were not, of course, confined to trade and manufacture. Any discussion of its sources of livelihood must also take account of its roles as a centre of *road communications* and in *local administration*. For many travellers it was a necessary staging-post when passing out of Wales towards London or from the Midlands to Bristol. By 1455 it had at least 10 inns, most notably the New Inn in Northgate Street which had recently been rebuilt on a substantial scale by Gloucester Abbey. Many people from the county had often to visit the town, which was the venue for all kinds of inquisitions and royal commissions, as well as the seat of the county administration and courts, which were duplicated after the 1483 charter made Gloucester and the adjoining hundreds of Dudstone and King's Barton into a separate county.

The amount of legal and other business transacted in the town and in connexion with its many religious houses is reflected in the number of lawyers who were prominent in Gloucester's affairs in the period. They included, in the early years of the 15th century, Robert Gilbert, who married the widow of John Banbury, the wealthy merchant mentioned earlier. Gilbert played a prominent part in the town government, and also held the post of steward of Llanthony Priory's estates. A similar example in a later age was Walter Rowden (d. 1514), three times mayor of Gloucester and steward of Gloucester Abbey's extensive manors. Other Gloucester lawyers of the period were essentially county gentry but found it convenient — for business purposes and to enable them to sit for the borough in Parliament — to maintain residences in the town and serve borough offices. Such men included John Edwards who in the 1440s became lord of the manor of Rodmarton (where the church still has his brass, depicting him in lawyer's robes) and, most notably, Sir William Nottingham who was appointed attorney-general in 1451 and who amassed considerable estates in the county.

Briefly described and evaluated have been Gloucester's main sources of livelihood in the later Middle Ages. Finally, an attempt has to be made at a general assessment of the state of the town's economy at the period. Unfortunately, the documentation necessary to make a worthwhile assessment — that is in particular good runs of the annual accounts of the bailiffs and the stewards, of the freemen's entry rolls, and of the rolls of unfranchised traders — do not survive. Gloucester will not, therefore, be one of the key places in determining the current debate among urban historians about the fortunes of English towns at the period. What we do have that might possibly make some contribution is a good collection of property deeds and leases, mainly in the unpublished registers of Gloucester Abbey and Llanthony Priory, and a careful analysis of those might prove a worthwhile exercise. We are left, meanwhile, to draw what conclusions we can from a random collection of evidence from a variety of other local and national sources.

The most obviously relevant evidence on the question of the prosperity of late-medieval Gloucester is a series of statements addressed by the townspeople to the central government. In 1447 they appealed to the Crown for aid, saying that the town was depopulated by plague and that hardly £40 of the annual fee-farm of £60 owed to the Crown could be collected. In 1455, when seeking powers to pave the streets, they spoke of their great poverty. In the negotiations that led to the granting of the 1483 charter they evidently made similar complaints, for they were excused the greater part of the fee-farm. In 1487 or 1488 (after Henry VII had restored the farm to its full amount) they petitioned for a reduction of the farm, claiming that 300 houses in the town were in decay, that their walls and bridges were in disrepair and that many of the wealthier inhabitants had left to avoid serving the office of sheriff; the two sheriffs (bailiffs before 1483) were responsible for payment of the farm and a decline in the revenues from which it was drawn — tolls charged on traders, landgavel rents, and fines levied in the borough court — had to be made up out of their own pockets. Finally, in 1505, when defending their claim to levy tolls on the river trade in the case mentioned above, the burgesses spoke of the decay of the town and of the difficulty in meeting the burden of repairs to public structures.

This evidence, apparently so conclusive, must be used with caution because of its context. In attempts to gain financial relief from the central government it was obviously desirable to paint as black a picture as possible. Such complaints from towns are fairly common at the period, particularly in connexion with their fee-farms, and there appears to have been almost a set formula for making them. In the 1505 suit over tolls, the final petitions of Gloucester and of its fellow-defendant, Worcester, were couched in almost identical terms. Nor were the petitioners always above deliberate manipulation of the facts: in 1455 the Gloucester burgesses said that they had no communal property that they could use to finance the paving work, whereas the community had by then acquired a substantial holding of houses in the town.

The evidence of the various appeals cannot, however, be discounted, and there are other indications of a decline in prosperity in the middle and later years of the 15th century. The early years of our period, from about 1380 to 1420, were evidently a reasonably prosperous time. The records of those years reveal a small but wealthy group of leading townsmen, mostly drapers and merchants, who monopolised the office of bailiff, bought up property in the town and the surrounding area, and endowed cchantries in the parish churches. By contrast, the records of the middle years of the 15th century provide very little evidence for such wealthy trading burgesses. The men of the earlier generation did not establish 'dynasties' and for the most part their surnames disappear from the lists of bailiffs; deterred presumably by the financial burden that the decline of the fee-farm revenues imposed on its holders, few now sought that office. Two other more concrete pieces of evidence that could be advanced for such a slump in prosperity are the reduction in the number of unfranchised traders indicated by the roll of 1481 — 108 people were listed compared to 285 in 1396 and *c.* 252 in 1423 — and the fact that the stewards' accounts for 1493 record that one quarter of the rents from the communal property in the town had lapsed. It would be unwise, however, to set too much store on the evidence of those two isolated survivals out of annual runs of records.

Out of such fragments that have by chance come down to us from a great mass of documents the historian tries to devise a coherent account of the economic fortunes of the late-medieval town. He is tempted to use in his argument everything that has survived, simply because it has survived, and the unrelated fragments can sometimes be assembled in different combinations to support quite different conclusions. We know, for example, that in this late-medieval period the burgess community carried on vigorously, and occasionally violently, disputes with the two large monastic houses, St. Peter's Abbey and Llanthony Priory, over questions of jurisdiction in the town; that on several occasions it was involved in disputes with other towns over the levying of tolls on traders; and that it took steps to enforce the usual protective measures which gave trading advantages to its freemen. We might cite these facts in one argument as evidence of the chronic insecurity that comes from the awareness of economic decline, or in another as manifestations of the vigour and self-confidence of a prosperous governing class. In the absence of full sources, historians of medieval towns build unsteady structures of argument, mortaring them together with such useful terms as 'apparently', 'probably' and 'it would seem that', well aware that the discovery of just a few different pieces of evidence could involve them in a complete rebuilding.

However, some sort of conclusion to this account of the economic history of late-medieval Gloucester is required. The conclusion offered here is that the town did experience a slump in prosperity in the middle and late 15th century, but one that was less catastrophic than the statements of the townspeople would suggest. The variety and the importance to its region of Gloucester's functions in trade, industry, local administration and communications made it less vulnerable than many towns to the economic problems of the day. It survived a difficult 60 years or so, to enjoy a resurgence in its fortunes in the early 16th century, a resurgence aided perhaps by the development of the capping industry and a revival of the corn trade. In 1524 Gloucester ranked 17th in the league table of English towns, much the same position as it had occupied at the start of our period; it was rated 15th in 1377. In terms of wealth and population it was well behind the great provincial centres of late-medieval England, like Norwich and Bristol, but it still occupied a respectable place among the county towns. The next 150 years would bring a more prolonged decline in its fortunes. In the 1520s, however, its economic performance did not appear too incongruously out of keeping with the impressive liberties that had been conferred upon it by its charter of 1483.

AUTHOR'S NOTE

The above account is based on parts of a chapter on 'Medieval Glouces-ter' which will be published in the forthcoming volume on Gloucester City in the *Victoria History of Gloucestershire* (Volume IV in the county set). The *History* is a joint project of Gloucestershire County Council and London University.

The main sources used for the above account include, from the

Gloucester borough records, five rolls listing unfranchised traders (Glos. Record Office, G.B.R., C 9/1-5); a freeman's register from 1535 (G.B.R., C 9/6); a hundred court book for 1502-7 (G.B.R., 1437/1559); a council memoranda book from 1486 (G.B.R., B 2/1); and a rental of the town, published as *Rental of all the Houses in Gloucester, A.D. 1455*, ed. W. H. Stevenson (1890). The 1505 suit over tolls is published in *Select Cases in Star Chamber* (Selden Soc. xvi), 209-26; (xxv), 285-7. Other information is taken from *Calendar of Patent Rolls; Calendar of Close Rolls; Rolls of Parliament*; the Gloucester Abbey registers (in Gloucester Cathedral Library); the Llanthony Priory registers (in Public Record Office, C 115); and P.C.C. wills of Gloucester burgesses (transcripts in 'Hockaday Abstracts' at Gloucester Divisional Library).

II

RICHARD III — KING OR ANTI-KING?

In January 1835 the first attempt was made to assassinate an American President — Andrew Jackson, seventh President of the United States. Jackson had gone to the famous white rotunda of the Capitol in Washington to attend the funeral of the Representative from South Carolina, Congressman Warren R. Davis, a man who was to become more famous in death than he ever was in life. As the President filed past the casket, a figure some six feet away drew a pistol and fired point-blank at the frail Jackson. The report echoed deafeningly in the rotunda, but the pistol had misfired. The would-be assassin, Richard Laurence, pulled out a second pistol; once more the cap exploded but again the pistol misfired. Jackson, who was naturally uninjured, lunged at Laurence with his cane — as one might expect of the first westerner ever to become President — but fortunately a young army officer reached him first and subdued him with the help of Davy Crocket. Laurence claimed at his trial that he was Richard III and rightfully king of England, and that Jackson somehow was barring his path to the throne. Accordingly, he was declared insane, acquitted and consigned to a mental asylum for life.

This incident has no great lasting significance, but it is not without some relevance to my theme. In 1835 Richard III was regarded as the embodiment of evil, if only by the diseased mind of a madman; Crocket later declared, 'I wanted to see the damnedest villain in this world — and now I have'. Moreover, the symbol of evil was foiled in his design by what some newspapers at the time regarded as God's protective hand: this conviction was strengthened by the evidence of a small arms expert who declared that the odds on two pistols misfiring in precisely the same way within seconds of one other were 125,000 : 1. This is a minor but instructive episode in the development of the posthumous reputation of Richard III in the English-speaking world.

29

During the fifteenth century, three separate dynasties occupied the English throne: the Lancastrians (1399-1461), the Yorkists (1461-85) and the Tudors (from 1485 onwards). Indeed, if one were allowed to appropriate the year 1399, one could raise the number to four, for the Plantagenet dynasty ended with the deposition of Richard II in 1399 and his murder the following year. No other century in English history has experienced such kaleidoscopic dynastic changes, except the eleventh century, when Anglo-Saxon, Danish and Norman houses monopolised the English throne. But not even the most short-lived of those, the Danish house, retained the crown for so short and fitful a period as did the Yorkists. They were probably the briefest of the ruling dynasties in the medieval history of western Europe.

The significance of these dynastic changes was profound, not least in precipitating a series of civil wars, the Wars of the Roses (1450-1500); and the Yorkist dynasty lay at their very heart — and not simply in terms of chronology. It was not a question, as it was in the eleventh century, of success or defeat for distinct cultural and political traditions: in the fifteenth century all three dynasties were indelibly English (even, it must be admitted, the Tudor dynasty), and all could claim a common descent from King Edward III (died 1377). Nevertheless, the dynastic changes in the fifteenth century were at least as bloody as those of the eleventh; in fact, then only one had come to a violent end (at Hastings), while both Lancastrian and Yorkist lines were truncated by violence — by the probable murders of King Henry VI and his son, and Edward V and his brother, and by the slaying of Richard III. And the Yorkists themselves appear to have been responsible for four out of five of those untimely deaths, Richard III for two of them and many say for all four.

This is all the more striking when it is recalled that all three dynasties embodied a monarchy that was more powerful and secure as an institution than that of the eleventh century, not least by the adoption of some clearer principles governing the hereditary descent of the crown in most circumstances; and by the creation of a religious, mystical aura about the kingship that went beyond mere ceremonial — beyond dropping to the knee in the presence of the king (which Richard II encouraged), beyond the fashion for the use of 'Majesty' as an address (which became popular during the fifteenth century), and beyond the faith that was placed in the royal touch as a cure for the skin disease, scrofula. Thus, the dynastic turbulence had its own remarkable quality — and at its heart stood the Yorkist kings. One is bound to ask how far they were responsible for that turbulence. It is more usual to blame the incompetent last Lancastrian king, Henry VI, but in 1471 Henry and his only son were killed, probably murdered. Why, then, did not the civil war end in 1471? Why did not the Yorkist dynasty survive for more than another fourteen years? In searching for an answer to these questions, one is bound to evaluate the responsibility of the two adult Yorkist kings themselves, Edward IV and his younger brother, Richard III, who was hacked to death at Bosworth Field on 22 August 1485 and with whose death the Yorkist dynasty came crashing down.

According to Charles Ross, 'Richard III has been the most persistently vilified of all English kings', more so even than 'Bad King John'. He is the only English king crowned since William the Conqueror not to have a tomb surviving today; even his nephews, 'The Princes in the Tower' (one of them the uncrowned Edward V), have a commemorative slab in Westminster Abbey, and King John lies in state in Worcester Cathedral. The reasons are well appreciated. Richard was a casualty partly of historical circumstances and partly of historiographical developments. He was defeated and slain in battle — the first English king to be so since 1066 — and to contemporaries that seemed to be a sign of God's condemnation. Moreover, he and his line were succeeded by the Tudors, who lasted five times as long as the Yorkists and had striking achievements to their credit which put Yorkist England in the shade. Tudor rule also coincided with the Renaissance, humanistic revolution in the writing of English history, which was turned to serve the splendid dramatic and persuasive reconstructions of Shakespeare. *Henry VI, Part Three* (in which his portrait of Richard was first revealed) was written in about 1590/1, and *Richard III* itself followed some months later in 1591.

It is doubtful if the damning view of Richard that resulted and which has been entrenched since the sixteenth century can ever be expunged from the consciousness of Englishmen — so ingrained is it in the popular conception of the development of England's story. Richard III is the only English king to cause extraordinary delusions in individuals which have inspired — and still inspire — destructive, violent, evil acts. The attempted assassination of Andrew Jackson is one such. More tragic still has been the report within recent months of the trial of a young man in Britain who murdered his fiancée: he too claimed that he had acted because he believed himself to be Richard III.

Since the beginning of the seventeenth century, there have been efforts made to modify the verdict of the sixteenth century. There has developed a long and tenacious line of rehabilitators of King Richard's reputation who are still as vigorous as ever, though some rather perverse and impervious to argument. In present-day historical studies, the most zealous members of this extraordinary phenomenon belong to a society known at its foundation in 1924 as the *Fellowship of the White Boar*, but which now operates under the more sober sobriquet of *The Richard III Society* — a change of title that perhaps emphasises the somewhat more serious and realistic methods now being used to achieve its unexceptionable aims:

> to secure a re-assessment of the material relating to this period, and of the role in English history of this monarch.

Such attention has ensured that Richard is the only English monarch to be celebrated regularly and publicly with vehement devotion: statues are erected to his memory, religious services are held in his name, sponsored publications elucidate his reign, and (the ultimate accolade) a royal patron has been enlisted for his *Society*. Not even St. Edward the Confessor, or the near-sainted Henry VI or yet Victoria the Queen-Empress occupies such a niche in the late-twentieth-century mind. Like no other English ruler, Richard III is today regarded as the embodiment of evil and yet, on the other hand, a worthy subject for determined rehabilitation.

Historical anniversaries ordinarily work wonders for the reputation of the person or event celebrated. The five hundredth anniversary of Richard's accession in 1483 is an exception — yet another of those extraordinary exceptions which he has inspired over the centuries. Two recent authoritative biographies of the king give no comfort to the devotees of his memory; on the contrary, they are more likely to outrage them. In 1981 there appeared Charles Ross's *Richard III*, in which the king appears as ruthless, arbitrary and violent, exhibiting a distressing lack of principle and a willingness to resort to secrecy and dissimulation to gain his ends. Desmond Seward's study appeared more appropriately in 1983; its subtitle, 'England's Black Legend', is the prelude to a boast that 'This is the most hostile life of Richard III to appear for over a century'. It claims that he was 'the most terrifying man ever to occupy the English throne, not excepting his great-nephew Henry VIII', and that 'His short life was filled by intrigue and slaughter . . .'. It is worth noting, too, that in 1981 the carefully annotated and authoritative Arden Edition of Shakespeare's famous play was published, with its compelling portrayal of the Royal Beast.

There is much to be said for these various views, especially those of Charles Ross, who detected strong indications that Richard's actions shocked many of his own subjects and led them to distrust, fear, even hate him. And contemporaries during his own lifetime — as opposed to sixteenth-century detractors — found him repulsive. All this is true and convincing up to a point, but two witnesses thought otherwise; these are usually noted only to be dismissed, but they deserve a more patient hearing. The first is Thomas Langton, bishop of St. David's.

Two weeks after his coronation, King Richard embarked on a tour or progress of his kingdom. He left Windsor Castle on 20 July 1483, made his way to Oxford, and then travelled on to Gloucester (where the townsmen importuned him for a charter that was granted formally later in the year), Tewkesbury, Warwick and points further north. Bishop Langton went with him; indeed, at Gloucester Langton was closer to his see than he was ever to be again. Richard had nominated him to St. David's whilst he was duke of Gloucester and protector of England after the death of Edward IV on 9 April 1483; a week after his own accession on the following 26 June, Richard confirmed the bishop's appointment. Whilst still on progress with the king, in September Langton wrote to his friend and confidant, the prior of Christ Church, Canterbury, William Sellyng; in the letter he gave his impressions of Richard and his bearing as king during the first few months of the reign and whilst he was on progress:

> He contents the people where he goes best that ever did [a] prince, for many a poor man that hath suffered wrong many days have been relieved and helped by him and his commands in his progress. And in many great cities and towns were great sums of money given him which he hath refused. On my truth, I never liked the conditions of any prince so well as his. God hath sent him to us for the weal of us all . . . Sensual pleasure holds sway to an increasing extent, but I do not consider that this detracts from what I have said.

Langton, then, painted a picture of a king who was concerned to help the disadvantaged and the poor seeking justice, who helped them swiftly and decisively and who thereby became popular. He records, too, a king who had the good will of the cities and towns he visited, but who refused to capitalise on this by taking the large gifts he was offered. Langton evidently admired Richard and his behaviour as king, even though he had doubts about the sensuality of his court.

The bishop's testimony is usually dismissed on the grounds that Langton was not an impartial observer. He came from Appleby (in Westmorland) and seems to have been one of the northerners whom Richard got to know in the 1470s when he lived and served Edward IV in the north of England; in any case (it is said), he was appointed by Richard himself to his bishopric in 1483. This is true, but there was more to Langton than that — and perhaps to Richard III. Langton was nowhere near the capital in the late summer of 1483 to have his attitudes conditioned by the rumours and fears that were spreading as a result of the deposition and imprisonment of the two young sons of Edward IV (including his heir, Edward V). Moreover, the bishop was highly intelligent and very well educated. Richard's testimonial to the Pope in December 1484, when the king promoted Langton to the see of Salisbury, spoke of his 'laudable merites, high vertues and profound [learning]'. In July 1483 he was corresponding with William Sellyng, who was nobody's fool: both men had studied in Italy and Sellyng was one of the most distinguished ornaments of the English Renaissance. They knew one another well, and Langton was unlikely to do other than write the truth as he saw it in a private letter to a close friend, especially one living in Canterbury, where he would certainly have opportunity to observe and learn about the king for himself. Langton's willingness to include in his letter some criticism of the royal court bears this out: his is no partisan assessment. Aside from that, Langton's abilities had been recognised some years earlier by Edward IV, whom he had served as a diplomat and chaplain; he was, too, valued later by Henry VII, who utilised Langton's diplomatic skills and promoted him first to the see of Winchester and then, in January 1501, to Canterbury itself (though Langton died of plague before the formalities could be completed). Even more significant, perhaps, was the goodwill shown him by Henry VII's queen, Elizabeth of York, who gave him a gift; she is hardly likely to have done this if he had been a partisan supporter of her brothers' murderer.

Is it possible to verify Langton's impressions of Richard's kingship — particularly the legal aid he offered to the poor and his anxiety to ease Englishmen's financial burdens — using other people's impressions and such objective evidence as the records of government provide? Earlier kings had been sensitive to the difficulties experienced by poor men in endeavouring to use complicated and expensive legal procedures. But Richard took a significant step in his first months as king to make life easier for such men, and no doubt the close contacts he had with his subjects while on progress were crucial. In December 1483 he accordingly designated formally a special clerk of his council, John Harrington, to continue his work in collecting, classifying and channelling requests and petitions from the poor and to submit them to councillors who sat for the purpose in the White Hall of the palace at Westminster. Richard III did take steps to ease poor men's burdens. Other evidence reveals that he was equally anxious to enable his subjects to complain when necessary against extortionate and oppressive officials, especially royal officials, and once again it may be that his progress led him to appreciate their problems all the more clearly.

It is known that Richard did decline money offered him by a number of towns, including Gloucester, Worcester, London and Canterbury. Moreover, on his visit to Gloucester at the end of July 1483 he agreed to give £20 per annum to St. Peter's Abbey, and much more to Tewkesbury where his brother Clarence was buried. When Parliament met in January 1484, its most important act was to outlaw arbitrary taxes of the sort that Edward IV had imposed and euphemistically termed 'benevolences'. Thus, when Richard himself sought loans in February 1485, he was well placed to ask for them, and he did so with a courtesy and a promise of repayment that Edward IV had rarely shown and offered:

> Sir, the king's grace greeteth you well, and desireth and heartily prayeth you that by way of loan, ye will let him have such sum as his grace hath written to you for; and ye shall truly have it again at such days as he had showed and promised to you in his letters, and this he desireth to be employed for the defence and surety of his royal person and the welfare of this his realm; and for that intent, his grace and all his lords think that every true Englishman will help him in this behalf, of which number his grace reputeth and taketh you for one; and that is the cause he this writeth to you before other for the great love, confidence and substance that his grace hath and knoweth in you which trusteth undoubtedly that ye, like a loving subject, will at this time accomplish this his desire.

Richard has received less than justice for the care he showed in handling his subjects, including the most humble of them. Indeed, he comes close to fulfilling one of the four clauses of the coronation oath that he swore in July 1483.

> Sire, will you in all your judgements have impartial and proper justice and discretion done in compassion and truth to the best of your ability?

Recent biographers maintain that if he ruled well it was only because it was politic to do so and that he dared do no other. Yet rulers, medieval and modern, are judged on the principles by which they act and the success with which they are able to translate these principles into actions. Their private reasons for adopting such principles — whether they be to keep a throne or win an election — seem less relevant. It is only equitable to judge Richard III on the same terms.

The second witness to Richard's rule is John Rous of Warwick. Rous probably saw — possibly met — King Richard during the progress of 1483, for in August the king arrived in Warwick. Rous had been born in Warwick, and spent most of his life there (he died in 1491) as chaplain of the chapel at Guy's Cliff, some two miles from the town on the river Avon. He was devoted to Warwick and its earls, who had founded and patronised the chapel in the fifteenth century. Rous was university educated, well read and the owner of a large library; he wrote a good deal of history — local, family, town and general — and he was no mean artist, to judge by the portrait drawings he included in some of his works.

Among these were two historical and genealogical rolls of the earls of Warwick, which seem to have been finished early in Richard IIIs reign; one may even have been presented to the king when he visited Warwick. They included a portrait of the king (who had married one of the daughters and heiresses of Richard Neville, earl of Warwick) and an assessment of the early months of his reign:

> The most mighty prince Richard by the grace of God king of England and of France and lord of Ireland by true matrimony without discontinuance or any defiling in the law, by heir male descending from King Harry the Second, all avarice set aside, ruled his subjects in his realm full commendably, punishing offenders by his laws, especially extortioners and oppressors of his commons, and cherishing tho[se] that were virtuous; by the which discreet guiding he got great thank of God and love of all his subjects rich and poor and great praise of the people of all other lands about him.

It is an eulogy and in part it repeats Richard's own publicised justification for seizing the throne from Edward IV's son. But significant, too, are those aspects of Richard's early reign which John Rous emphasised, especially in view of Bishop Langton's private and quite independent letter composed at about the same time. To Rous, Richard appeared not to be avaricious; he was concerned to offer justice, especially against those who were extortionate and oppressive towards the common folk; and he was popular with rich and poor alike.

John Rous's testimony is usually dismissed because after the battle of Bosworth he expunged from one of his genealogical rolls his assessment of the defeated monarch, and because, in his *History of the Kings of England*, completed after 1485, he gave a quite different and much more hostile verdict on Richard III. In this revised version, Richard appeared as the Anti-Christ, a man horrifically born, with a distasteful deformity, who poisoned his wife in order to marry his niece; whereas Henry VII appeared as God's messenger and God's instrument. Anyone who would change his mind so completely, it is usually argued, must be unreliable in all he writes. Yet, even in the most hostile portrait, Rous felt moved to add one or two significant colours:

> The money which was offered him by the peoples of London, Gloucester and Worcester he declined with thanks, affirming that he would rather have their love than their treasure.

And of Richard at Bosworth itself, he wrote:

> If I would speak the truth in his honour, I must say that he bore himself with great distinction like a noble knight despite his small body and slight strength, most honourably defending himself to his last breath.

These two witnesses, the one openly, the other despite himself after 1485, suggest a king who strove to be a fit and proper ruler — and with some success. But this was Richard after his usurpation of the English throne.

When Edward IV died on 9 April 1483, England faced only its fourth royal minority since the Norman Conquest. The previous three had been weathered reasonably successfully, with the surviving brothers of the late king occupying an honoured place; and the three earlier minor kings had been considerably younger than Edward V, who was twelve when his father died in 1483. The present minority may usefully be compared with that of Henry VI in 1422: two usurping dynasties were faced with a minority after twenty-two or -three years, and after ten or twelve years of stable, successful government. And in 1422, there were two royal brothers at the disposal of the dynasty and the baby king, not simply one as in 1483. Yet in June 1483 the brother of the late king, Richard of Gloucester, deposed his young nephew and seized his throne.

All the signs are that the sons of Richard, duke of York — Edward IV, George of Clarence and Richard of Gloucester — acted more like ambitious, overmighty magnates, with aristocratic horizons rather than royal ones. They committed deliberate, destructive acts against their own dynasty in 1469 and 1483, and even some of Edward IV's acts as king were ruthless and illegal. The Crowland Chronicler seems to have known all three (my italics):

> These three brothers . . . were possessed of such surpassing talents that, *if they had only been able to live without dissension*, such a threefold cord could never have been broken without the utmost difficulty.

37

In 1483 Richard of Gloucester was unwilling to rest content with the role of uncle of the new king and protector of his realm, even though he was Edward V's sole royal uncle (unlike the situation in 1377 and 1422). It is true that he did not have custody of the person of the young king; but he could hardly expect it, since to combine custody of the king and custody of the realm in one person was not the custom in England. Still, it must be admitted that the boy-king was now in the hands of the powerful faction of his mother, which was certain to be distrustful of Richard of Gloucester. It is true that Richard did not have the position of regent of England; but that was un-English too and had already been rejected twice in the fifteenth century as inappropriate in England. On the other hand, Richard became protector of the realm, as he could reasonably expect to be as Edward IV's sole surviving brother; though admittedly, with the new king aged twelve he could not expect to hold the position for long. On the other hand, also, he was Edward V's only surviving uncle on his father's side; though the memory of that other duke of Gloucester who was the sole surviving royal uncle of Henry VI after 1435 might well have been in his mind — for Humphrey, duke of Gloucester had been ignored, victimised and humiliated despite his position. Yet in spite of all, it must be said that a loyal subject and upholder of his family and dynasty would have — nay, should have — accepted his position and the realities of Yorkist politics, no matter how uncomfortable these might be. In explaining why he did not do so, the matter of Richard's personality, character and ambition bulks large.

The explanation — it can hardly be a justification — lay in his concern for his personal position and the established habits of ruthlessness and illegality of the Yorkist family and Yorkist régime. After all, unlike the situation in 1399 and 1461, the young king in 1483 could in no sense be regarded as deserving deposition, let alone captivity and death in the Tower of London.

Richard III went far towards demolishing the Yorkist monarchy of which he himself was a part. He eliminated the main line by deposing Edward V and probably murdering him and his young brother Richard in the Tower, and by the stories he circulated about their birth and even about their father's birth. He ignored the secondary line of his older brother George of Clarence, though Clarence's son and daughter still lived. Richard's actions and methods in 1483 turned men's minds to alternative possibilities as king; even staunch defenders of the Yorkist monarchy like Edward IV's widow, Queen Elizabeth Woodville, and Edward's old officers were prepared to contemplate these alternatives too. In that sense, Richard had become Anti-King.

Richard's actions and methods precipitated a defence of the Yorkist monarchy that was directed against himself, and on to that movement of defence was grafted an alternative dynastic claim, ultimately represented by Henry Tudor. No amount of demonstration of sound government and laudable instincts as a ruler could remove the fundamentally damaging fact that on no reasonable ground — reasonable in the fifteeenth-century mind — ought Richard to have been king.

AUTHORITIES

For the attempted assassination of President Jackson, see J.W. Clarke, *American Assassinations*: *The Darker Side of Politics* (1982). The most recent biographies of Richard III are Charles Ross, *Richard III* (1981), and Desmond Seward, *Richard III: England's Black Legend* (1983); the best edition of Shakespeare's play is *Richard III* (Arden ed., 1981). The Richard III Society produces a quarterly *Bulletin* of chit-chat of interest only to members of the Society, but its journal, *The Ricardian*, often contains historical material of value. Thomas Langton's letter is printed in J.B. Sheppard (ed.), *Christ Church Letters* (Camden Society, 1877), p.45, and translated best in A.R. Myers (ed.), *English Historical Documents*, vol. IV (1327–1485) (1969), pp. 336–7; the details of his career are usefully listed in A.B. Emden, *A Biographical Register of the University of Oxford to A.D. 1500*, vol. II (1958), pp. 1101–2; for the intellectual circle in which he and Sellyng moved, see R. Weiss, *Humanism in England during the Fifteenth Century* (1941). For John Rous and his genealogical rolls, see Charles Ross (ed.), *The Rous Roll* (1980, reprinting the 1859 ed.), which prints the eulogy of Richard III; the *History of the Kings of England* is in T. Hearne (ed.), *Joannis Rossi Antiquarii Warwicensis Historia Regum Anglie* (1716), though the hostile account of the king is also translated in A. Hanham, *Richard III and his Early Historians, 1483–1535* (1975), pp. 118—24. Records of Richard's administration include *Calendar of Patent Rolls, 1476–85* (especially p. 413); *Statutes of the Realm*, vol. II, p. 478 (1484), and R. Horrox and P.W. Hammond (eds.), *British Library, Harleian Manuscript 433* (3 vols., 1979–82), with my quotation from vol. III, p. 130.
Related authoritative studies include J.R. Lander, *Conflict and Stability in Fifteenth Century England* (3rd. paperback ed., 1977); Ralph A. Griffiths, *The Reign of King Henry VI* (1981); Charles Ross, *Edward IV* (1974); and S.B. Chrimes, *Henry VII* (1972).

III

1483: GLOUCESTER AND TOWN GOVERNMENT IN THE MIDDLE AGES

The obvious and appropriate way to start my talk is by congratulating you. I congratulate you on the five hundredth anniversary of your charter and on choosing to celebrate it. It is not, if you do not mind my saying so, that Gloucester is exceptionally old among the county towns of England or that the charter of 1483 was very exceptional among fifteenth-century town charters. That does not in my view detract from the importance or pleasantness of the occasion: Gloucester and its charter are both good and representative examples of good and interesting phenomena and therefore worth a bit of corporate civic celebration. What makes the occasion unusual and pleasing to an historian is that you are celebrating an event of real significance in your history, and that your celebrations include a real effort to find out what happened and why it was significant. Some towns, I am afraid, choose to boast of fictitious or semi-fictitious events — mythical foundations, or imaginary charters supposedly granted by impossibly early kings, and do not seem to worry about the nonsense they make of history. Others which resist the temptation to improvise the past are unlucky in not happening to have any single charter that is particularly worth commemorating, but just a series, each saying very little that is different from the one before and providing only a rather dreary set of minor anniversaries, none of which is really worth celebrating.

1483, however, marked the biggest change for 300 years in the constitution of the town of Gloucester: I refer to it throughout, you may notice, not as a city but as a town or borough. Borough in medieval terms meant very much the same as town: its constitutional significance was very loose. 'City', on the other hand, was normally reserved to towns which were bishops' sees, so Gloucester did not become a city, in the usage of the time, until 1541, when the former abbey became a cathedral. Before that, in 1483, the town — or borough — got some useful new privileges and an amended and more clearly defined constitution. In order to appreciate what this meant we need to go back to see how the government of the town had developed since the twelfth century, and we also need to do something more difficult. We must try to forget the political arrangements and language and ideas of today and think ourselves through the words of the charter into the minds of the medieval burgesses (not citizens) of Gloucester and see what they expected of their municipal government, why they wanted a new charter, and what was the point of its various provisions.

During the twelfth and thirteenth centuries the kings of England granted many towns a measure of self-government. Generally speaking most of the larger towns, including most of the county towns, like Gloucester, secured what was called the 'farm' (or by the fifteenth-century the 'fee-farm') of the borough: that is, the right to appoint their own officials who would then be responsible for paying over the town's dues and taxes to the royal exchequer each year. That did not exempt the town from fairly frequent interference from the central government: something very like the present-day complaints of local councillors and officials about Whitehall could have been heard in the guildhalls of medieval England, and rather fiercer language was used in the royal letters they received than, I imagine, appears in most of the letters from Whitehall today. Nevertheless, though the grant of 'the farm of the borough' did not mean total independence, it did mean that towns-people henceforth elected their own officials and councillors freely, and generally looked after their own everyday affairs. The chief reason why they valued this privilege was not that it gave them the right to consult together and act corporately. They already had that: all government, whether of towns or any other units of government, was supposed to be conducted through meetings or courts which dealt with political, administrative, and judicial matters, all mixed up together. Normally a representative of the king or lord would preside — in the case of Gloucester, the king's reeve — but decisions and judgements were supposed to be made by a consensus of the more important members of the community, who were supposed to represent the whole. The advantage of getting the 'farm of the borough' was that now the townsmen had more freedom of decision in their meetings: they chose their own officers who would lead their collective deliberations, and they could hold meetings as and when they wanted, raise money for themselves, and spend it how they liked — more or less. Above all, their officers could represent them in dealing with the central government and could bargain on their behalf about dues and taxes. Bargain is the key word: the whole system involved a great deal of negotiation. It could suit a king very well to delegate local authority direct to local communities and to allow them a good deal of independence, provided that they collected and paid over royal taxes and generally behaved in a reasonably law-abiding and obedient way. Sometimes therefore towns secured privileges with very little trouble. Sometimes, however, depending on the incalculable — and to us, usually unknowable — combination of political pressures, personalities, and local circumstances, a bit more effort was needed — oiling some palms at court, maybe, or even a spot of rebellion and rioting.

Surviving medieval records are generally too formal and gnomic to tell just how and why individual towns achieved their successes, but, for Gloucester they are just good enough to reveal an outline, if rather a hazy outline, of the main stages by which its government developed — or rather they are good enough to reveal it to people as expert and indefatigable in reading them as the staff of the *Victoria County Histories*. You have already heard Dr. Herbert's lecture, so you will appreciate how much he knows about the town. I have to confess that the account I am about to give you draws heavily on the draft he has lent me of the chapters which will deal with the government of the medieval town in the *V.C.H.* volume on the city. When that comes out — I hope in not too many years from now — you will be able to check what I have said against the details and against a full battery of references to the original documents.[1]

The burgesses of Gloucester, like those of many other towns, secured their first charter from King Henry II in the mid-twelfth century. Like most of his charters to towns, however, Henry's charter to Gloucester was fairly limited in scope: it allowed them to have the same freedom from tolls as the citizens of London and Winchester, and to use the same legal procedures in their courts, and that was all. Later in his reign, however, from 1165 to 1176, the town's annual dues were paid into the royal exchequer separately from those of the rest of the county, and it looks as if the reeve who paid them was in effect doing so as the representative of the burgesses rather than as the king's servant. Maybe the position was not quite clear enough for the burgesses, however, because in 1170 some of them were slapped down and fined for forming a 'commune' — a word commonly used at the time to describe an association formed to campaign for collective rights. Six years later Gloucester was back under the sheriff — though we may note that the burgesses still accounted for some of their dues collectively and not through him. They must meanwhile, of course, have still been acting collectively under him in their town courts and assemblies. Anyway, like many other towns, they did better out of Henry II's two sons than out of the father. Richard I formally granted the 'farm of the borough of Gloucester' to its burgesses by charter, and in 1200 King John, in return for 200 marks (a mark was two-thirds of a pound), confirmed the grant and added various other privileges, like having all lawsuits about property in Gloucester, or about debts incurred there, tried within the town.

Just (we may feel) to make life more complicated for historians, John's charter refers first to 'our burgesses of Gloucester' and later to 'our burgesses of Gloucester of the merchants' guild'. Historians have tied themselves into knots over the possible distinction between burgesses and guildsmen, borough and guild. The general consensus seems to be that a merchant guild was generally a rather restricted and élite group, which stood for the interests of the richer townspeople against the interests of the rest. I am not sure that is right. In certain circumstances it might be, but it is clear, I think, that at Gloucester, as in many other towns, the guild was simply the association or body through which the town as a whole organized the commercial side of its affairs. The thirteenth-century municipal seal was inscribed 'Sigillum burgensium de gilda mercatorum Gloucestrie' — the seal of the burgesses of the guild of merchants of Gloucester — and in the fifteenth century those who became burgesses were sworn in as burgesses of the merchants' guild. The symbiosis of the two bodies may also explain a slight uncertainty about the relationship between the Boothall, off Westgate Street, and the guildhall. One thirteenth-century deed suggests that they may have been separate buildings, though standing close together, but more often, as I understand, the documents suggest that Boothall and guildhall were one and the same: a single building where town business of all sorts was conducted. Confusing as all this may seem to us, it caused little difficulty at the time, because medieval law allowed people to be very vague about their collective activities, about which people belonged to which group, or about which of their several capacities they were acting in at any given moment. Moreover, even the obvious fact that many inhabitants of the town may not have been traders at all would not have worried them: the leading burgesses whom everyone would expect to be the chief decision-makers and rulers of the town probably would be traders, and they were supposed to represent the interests of the whole community. This reliance on consensus is reflected in the final clauses of the 1200 charter. Here the king granted that the burgesses should by common consent choose two of the more lawful and discreet from their number to be reeves, who, so long as they behaved themselves, would not be removable except by consent of the town, and four of the more lawful and discreet to be coroners — an office which had much wider duties than it has today.

It was within the loose framework of this charter that Gloucester was governed until 1483. Apart from a short period in the early thirteenth century when a mayor was somehow grafted on to the local government hierarchy, the two reeves, or bailiffs as they came to be called, were in charge, apparently subject to annual election though often serving for three or four years or even longer. By the mid-fourteenth century there were also four annually elected stewards who looked after corporate funds, and we read too (or the *V.C.H.* editors read) of other officials who served the town at a humbler level: servants or under-bailiffs to empanel juries, summon defendants, and keep the prison; clerks to keep the records; and porters to keep the gates. All these are recorded because they were paid, but paid officials did not multiply as fast in medieval local government as in some later ages, because an enormous amount of work was done by the burgesses themselves without any pay: not just giving up their free time to serve on official councils and committees, and in voluntary societies and organizations, like their successors today; but assessing and collecting taxes, surveying municipal property, inspecting public works, and performing a host of other duties that are now too technical and complicated for any but fulltime career officials.

It was a very 'participatory' sort of government, but that does not mean that it was — or was meant to be — democratic. The bailiffs and coroners were elected, but that did not necessarily mean that they were elected by the equal votes of equal individuals, let alone that all the inhabitants of the town were electors. The right and duty to take part in the government of the town belonged only to the burgesses. Just who counted as a burgess we do not know for sure but by analogy with other towns I think we can say pretty definitely that the inhabitants of Gloucester would have taken it for granted that the burgesses would be resident householders who paid their share of the town's dues and taxes. That means that wives and children, living-in servants, and other dependants would be excluded as a matter of course, but so, apparently, were some householders. At Gloucester there were people called portmen, some at least of whom seem to have been householders resident in the town, who apparently ranked as members of the town community but not as full burgesses. By the fifteenth century you could become a burgess of Gloucester by making a down payment, or by serving an apprenticeship in the town, or by being the son of a burgess, and the names of those thus admitted to the franchise were sometimes written down. Yet at no time, either in Gloucester or so far as I know elsewhere, were full registers of burgesses kept. To us that seems extraordinary, but I think that we can begin to understand it if we recognise that medieval townspeople started from an attitude to government and politics which was in some ways completely different from ours.

All the collective and consultative practices which were so important in their government were designed to represent not a collection of individuals with equal and separate rights, but a community of different ranks, bound together by ties of due and lawful order and hierarchy. It was seen as the duty as well as the right of the richest and most senior burgesses to take the lead in government and to assume the heaviest responsibilities, though they were supposed to consult with the other burgesses when necessary. In consequence it did not really matter exactly who attended or had the right to attend meetings, provided that those who did so were solid and respectable people and that, when particularly important matters were to be discussed, a particularly large and representative number would turn up. Just as it was hoped that the 'more lawful and more discreet' would represent their humbler fellows fairly and would judge between them justly, so it was hoped that honest and wise men would agree about what was fair and just. Everyone knew, of course, that all men were sinners and that some were fools, so in practice they did not really expect to attain to the ideal of unanimity very often. That being so, consensus was second best to unanimity, with numerical majorities a poor third. To them a soggy consensus seemed better than a neat majority partly because it evened out differences of seniority and status: in reaching a consensus the opinion of the most respected participants — who were almost bound to include, and rightly include, the rich and powerful — would be especially influential. This explains, I think, why it was that on the rare occasions when townspeople tried to define the qualifications for the burgess franchise they were not primarily concerned about the political rights it entailed. What they were concerned about were the legal and economic privileges which the burgesses of Gloucester of the guild merchant enjoyed under their charters: freedom from tolls at Gloucester and elsewhere, and the right to have various sorts of law-suit tried only in their own courts. These rights were valuable, and maintaining them took both time and money. They therefore belonged only to fully paid-up members of the town community. That did not mean that only burgesses could trade in the town at all: apart from the portmen, who probably, in return for their

45

rather lower entry fees, enjoyed more restricted trading rights than the full burgesses, merchants from elsewhere came to buy and sell goods, while country people brought in food to sell to the townspeople. All of these outsiders however, had to pay tolls each time or an annual composition fee instead.

Against this background we can imagine Gloucester being run between 1200 and 1483 by the bailiffs and other officials through weekly meetings of the court, and perhaps other meetings as well, mostly held at the Boothall. Most of the time there would be only a relatively small number of burgesses present and most of them would be those hopefully described in the 1200 charter as the more lawful and more discreet: those rich enough to be able to leave their businesses, public-spirited enough to spare the time, and, maybe, some of them just the sort of people who like attending meetings and running things. Whether they ever constituted a formal council is unknown: some towns set up councils of twelve, or of multiples of twelve, to ensure that the officers had regular advice at hand, but some relied on the general body of burgesses to supervise the officers. Perhaps at Gloucester the jury which reported to the specially important sessions of the court which were held twice a year acted as some sort of council. In any event the normal practice should have been that once or twice a year, perhaps at these big court sessions, an extra full assembly of burgesses would meet, perhaps in the greater space of the street outside the Boothall, to hear the officers present their accounts and to elect new ones.

Human arrangements seldom work quite as they are meant to. The natural result of the respectful and hierarchical tendencies of that time was that government tended to be left to inner groups, and those inner groups sometimes succumbed to the temptations of their position. Their position *was* tempting, because their powers were wide and their tasks were complex. The regulation of a town's trade and industry involved trying to reconcile the interests of employers and employees, producers and retailers, retailers and consumers, visiting merchants and domestic producers. Considering that even with the help of economists and other experts modern governments find this sort of thing very difficult, it is not surprising that the rulers of medieval towns often got in a muddle and that recriminations flew around. In such circumstances it must have been tempting for leading townsmen, whose own private interests were inevitably involved, to ignore criticism and just do the best they could for themselves. Since they were also the people who did justice, dealt with complaints, and assessed and raised rates and taxes, and since the habit of trusting the 'more lawful and more discreet' was so ingrained, it was very easy for town governments to become corrupt. That seems to be what happened at Gloucester during the thirteenth century. In the 1270s one of the burgesses who served repeated terms as bailiff seems to have been among those who were accused of 'forestalling' — that is, buying up provisions (in his case fish) before they reached the open market. In 1290 the 'community of the town of Gloucester' complained to parliament that the powerful men of the town had often levied taxes from them without cause and, it was implied, had put the money they raised to improper uses.

We do not know what response was made to these complaints but, to judge from what is known of similar troubles elsewhere, it probably involved drawing up stricter rules to ensure that accounts would be regularly submitted to full and open meetings, and that elections would be regularly and openly conducted. So far as I know, no one in medieval times seems to have thought that it would help to change the structure of government radically. They continued to think that the best fitted to rule were the rich, and that if rulers did not succeed in reconciling all interests justly, that was not because of any inherent conflict of interests but because of sin. Before we conclude that this was naïve of them, we ought to notice that during the later middle ages, as rules were elaborated, and also, I think, as civic consciousness developed accordingly, their own remedies seem to have been working. Dangerous as it is to draw deductions from negative evidence in medieval history, it is worth noticing that, despite the growing volume of surviving records, we still have nothing from the fourteenth and fifteenth centuries which corresponds with the complaints of 1273 and 1290. I do not suggest that everyone who held office in late medieval Gloucester was impeccably and selflessly honourable and just, but we have no reason to suppose that any of them behaved in the corrupt and oligarchical way that some of their thirteenth-century predecessors had done.

What the evidence of the municipal records, as recounted by Dr. Herbert, suggests to me is that by the fifteenth century the bailiffs, stewards, and leading burgesses of Gloucester were becoming increasingly busy with all sorts of apparently public-spirited activities. In 1398 they had secured a charter which made the bailiffs into justices of the peace and slightly enlarged their jurisdiction in commercial cases. Meanwhile they were undertaking public works like repairing the walls, paving the streets, and building new mills on the river, and in 1438 they concluded an agreement with the local Franciscan friary to tap the friary's water-pipes so as to provide a public water supply. In order to pay for all this the town's financial officers, the stewards, could draw on the rents of an increasing amount of communal property. Apart from corporately owned buildings and lands, whose rents went to the common funds, the town by now also held other property in trust for hospitals and other charitable purposes. There was plenty for the bailiffs and stewards to do and, so far as we know, they were doing it fairly well.

Not that everything in the fifteenth century was perfect. Conditions in the country at large were very different from those in the days when Gloucester secured its first charter from King John and had its fee-farm fixed. The population of England had dropped dramatically in the fourteenth century and patterns of trade were changing. As a result a good many towns were smaller both in population and total wealth, and some of them complained loudly about having to pay the fee-farms and taxes that had been fixed in palmier days. Just what this tells us about their prosperity is difficult to judge: in some cases public poverty — or the poverty of the particular funds from which the fee-farms were traditionally paid — seems to have been compatible with a fair amount of private affluence.[2] How far that was the case at Gloucester Dr. Herbert may have been able to guess, but the town certainly petitioned for a reduction of its fee-farm in 1447. Financial worries are likely to have been an important motive for asking for a new charter in 1483.

Here, however, we are, as usual, in the realm of conjecture. We do not know anything about the negotiations for the charter except what can be deduced from its text and from what happened immediately afterwards.[3] The rest of my lecture will therefore consist of my deductions from that evidence. One preliminary point should be made: any charter to a town was granted in response to a request from the town. Political pressures might determine a king to grant or refuse the request, but the details of the grant, provided that they fell within the range which was acceptable to him and his advisers, would be of little concern to the king. They would reflect what the town asked. That is why I deduce that the burgesses of Gloucester were feeling a financial pinch – or at least a corporate financial pinch — in 1483: for the charter reduced their fee-farm from £65 to £20. Moreover, I suspect that a second provision of the charter also reflects financial concerns: that is, the making of Gloucester into a separate county, to which was added a sizable tract of neighbouring countryside, comprising the hundreds of Dudstone and King's Barton. This, however, was not desirable only for the additional income it would bring to the town and retain within it. Bristol had been made a separate county in 1373 for the practical reason that it lay on the borders of Somerset and Gloucestershire, so that its officers and inhabitants had to deal with two sets of county officials some distance away. For a county town such reasons did not apply, but Bristol had started a fashion, and by 1483 ten more grants of county status had been made to towns, including half a dozen county towns. There were municipal Joneses to be kept up with in fifteenth-century England.

Two other motives often prompted townsmen to ask for new charters at this time, and both apply to our case. Since the time of the first town charters legal learning and the legal profession had developed a great deal, and the law had consequently become more complex. Lawyers were beginning to worry about the corporate ownership of property and the problems which it could create for towns whose charters had been made in an age of legal innocence, when any group at all could own property and act collectively at law. Some towns were therefore finding it prudent — and their lawyers were no doubt finding it profitable — to have their right to own and manage municipal property explicitly set out in a charter. It looks as if that was the case at Gloucester, for the 1483 charter declares the burgesses a corporate body with the right to hold property and to sue and be sued in any court. One might therefore call it a 'charter of incorporation', but that is a bit misleading; Gloucester had been acting as a corporation for centuries and the clauses in the charter which declared it one were a precautionary afterthought, not a legal necessity.

The second common reason for wanting a new charter in the fifteenth century was that the authority of a royal charter could be a good way of making changes in a town's constitution. Change might be needed in order to end a conflict, in which case royal authority would help to overcome the resistance of the defeated party; or it might be simply that immemorial arrangements were being changed and resistance was feared from the more conservative townspeople. The constitutional provisions of the 1483 charter do not look as if they were designed to resolve conflict, and there is, as I have said, no evidence that there had recently been any at Gloucester; but they do look as though they were designed to bring the town's constitution up to date. Some other quite important towns, like Worcester, for instance, were still ruled by pairs of bailiffs, and some still had no formal councils, but those arrangements were beginning to look a little old-fashioned as others went over to the alternative constitution of a mayor, aldermen, and common council on the London model. That was what the ruling burgesses of Gloucester had evidently decided to do. At the same time as turning the two bailiffs into joint sheriffs of the new county, the charter replaced them at the head of the municipal hierarchy by a mayor, before whom a sword might be ceremonially carried in the town, and twelve aldermen. The charter did not expressly provide for an outer or common council in addition to the aldermen, but as a common council of forty (the officers, aldermen and 22 others) was in existence a year later, that was probably intended to be part of the package. Long and detailed as fifteenth-century charters were in comparison with those of the twelfth, they still had some surprising gaps: their form depended on what local people thought of and asked for.

In this case it is not at all clear that the local people had thought out all the possible implications of the arrangements they made. The first mayor and aldermen were to be elected by the burgesses, but thereafter the aldermen were to serve for life, filling vacancies by co-option, while mayors were to be elected each year by the aldermen and twelve other of the more lawful and discreet of the burgesses. Nothing was said about the way these extra twelve, or of course the unmentioned council, were to be elected. This vagueness, combined with the initial popular elections, suggests to me that the framers of the charter were not intending to restrict participation in government by the burgesses at large. I reckon that motives can be more accurately deduced from plans for the immediate future than from those for further off, for the long-term implications of human arrangements are seldom as clear to people at the time as to historians afterwards. If the new constitution had been deliberately intended to introduce a 'closed corporation' it would not have started with open elections or left so many loopholes for popular participation in the future. This part of the charter, therefore, confirms the impression that, so far as we know, the government of Gloucester was reasonably harmonious and efficient in the years leading up to 1483. The town authorities apparently felt no need to spell out safeguards against popular discontents or revolts any more than against official corruption or oppression. The remaining clauses of the charter — the appointment of a coroner for the new county, the position of the mayor and aldermen as J.Ps., the safeguarding of the toll-freedom of traders from Tewkesbury in Gloucester, and so on, need no special discussion. They all seem to me quite straightforward and compre-hensible.

The leading burgesses of Gloucester in 1483 had not only been — apparently — happy and efficient in running their town so far. They were now — apparently — happy and efficient in their negotiations with the central government — unless, of course, they had originally wanted a lot more than the charter actually gave them. But they could hardly have hoped for more on the financial front. Richard III not only remitted over two-thirds of the fee-farm, but granted the whole charter for nothing, because of 'the good and faithful actions of the bailiffs and burgesses in causes of particular importance to us' — that is, to him. Whether this refers to the help Gloucester had given to his brother Edward IV against the Lancastrian army in 1471, or to more recent help in his own reign, is unknown, at least to me. By September 1483 Richard had enough troubles of his own, I suspect, to be effusively grateful for support from anywhere. At any rate on 2 September 1483 Gloucester got its charter — though at this stage I should perhaps point out that strictly and pedantically speaking it was not actually a charter so much as letters patent. By this date the sort of documents which were originally called charters were going out of use: they were officially discontinued soon after in 1516. Letters patent came to the same thing and Gloucester's letter patent constituted a handsome grant. It reduced the town's financial liabilities, extended its jurisdiction and therefore its income, safeguarded its property, increased its civic dignity, and provided the outline of a more formal and regular system of consultation and election. How all this was to work in practice and how long the apparent harmony of 1483 was to last I leave to Peter Clark to tell you.

NOTES

1. Pending the publication of the *V.C.H.* for Gloucester, there is an English summary of the charters in W.H. Stevenson, *Calendar of the records of Gloucester* (Gloucester, 1893), 1–48. A fuller account of my interpretation of medieval urban history is given in S. Reynolds, *Introduction to the history of English medieval towns* (Oxford, 1977) and of the political ideas behind it in 'Medieval urban history and the history of political thought', *Urban History Yearbook 1982*, 14–26.
2. On this controversial subject see e.g. R.B. Dobson, 'Urban decline in late medieval England', *Trans. Royal Hist. Soc.* 5th series, xxvii (1977), 1–22; S Reynolds, 'Decline and decay in late medieval towns', *Urban History Yearbook 1980*, 76–8; A.R. Bridbury, 'English provincial towns in the fifteenth century', *Economic Hist. Rev.* 2nd series, xxxiv (1981), 1–24.
3. There does not appear to be any petition or warrant for the charter in the Public Record Office. I have searched PSO 1/56 and C 81/886, 1327, 1392, 1529, 1531 for warrants and no petition appears in the list of SC 8.

A POISONED CHALICE? THE 1483 CHARTER, THE CITY AND THE COUNTY 1483–1662

During Henry VIII's reign John Leland described the 'town of Gloucester' as 'ancient, well builded of timber and large, and strongly defended with walls'; to the quay on the left bank of the Severn 'picards and small boats come'. 'The beauty of the town [he went on] lies in two crossing streets as the gates of the town lie.'[1] At the close of the Middle Ages Gloucester probably had a population of 3–3,500 and was second only to Bristol in the shire. It held, of course, a major strategic position as the first easy crossing point above the Severn estuary and at the crossroads of north-south and east-west communication routes. As well as being an important market centre and river port, Gloucester was well known for its cloths, caps and metal trades. The numerous monastic houses — headed by the great abbey of St Peter's — attracted many visitors to town — tenants, pilgrims and others. Despite complaints of urban decay in the 15th and early 16th centuries, Gloucester seems to have been tolerably prosperous at the end of the medieval period — certainly compared with places like York, Canterbury, Oxford and Coventry which we know were in serious decline.[2]

Therefore Richard III's charter of incorporation, granted shortly after his visit to the town in early August 1483, was due recognition of Gloucester's status as one of the leading 20 towns in the kingdom. At the same time, the generosity of the charter, confirming old privileges and granting new ones, was not wholly altruistic. Richard at this time was busy trying to consolidate his political power, winning friends and neutralising enemies, through the lavish distribution of political favours. Gloucester was one of a number of urban beneficiaries.

However my task here is not to explore the background of the 1483 charter, but to look at its achievement. For while the granting of the charter may have been influenced by the short-term pressures of political expediency, the charter itself was to stand the test of time.

52

Though there were further grants of privileges by Henry VIII, Elizabeth and the early Stuart kings, Richard III's charter was to shape the political fortunes of the city for nearly two centuries, and to regulate the way the town was ruled for much longer.

Two aspects of the charter are of particular interest. Firstly the new framework it established (more or less explicitly) for civic government. After 1483 this was under the formal control of a mayor, bench of aldermen, two sheriffs, and common council, but with considerable and growing authority in the hands of the mayor and aldermen. Though towns had tended to be run by relatively small elites since the high middle ages if not before, from the late 15th century royal charters and parliamentary statutes encouraged the concentration of political power in the hands of a limited number of urban magnates. By the early 17th century the rise of civic oligarchy was a major development not only at Gloucester but in many English and continental cities. The reasons for the growth of oligarchy and its impact on town government — with the spread of corruption and conflict — will be one of the main themes of this lecture.

The other feature of the charter which had ramifying consequences for Gloucester politics and above all relations with the county was the provision that from Michaelmas 1483 the 30 or so villages and hamlets in the Hundreds of Dudston and King's Barton, at that time part of the shire, were to be incorporated along with Gloucester 'as the county of the town of Gloucester'. This was an almost unprecedented concession (only York had a similar extensive tract of countryside under its jurisdiction). For city magistrates it offered the prospect of controlling a large part of Gloucester's market hinterland, taxing the villages to the benefit of the urban community. But in the long run the annexation of the so-called inshire to Gloucester proved politically and economically damaging, spawning increasingly acrimonious disputes with landowners in the two hundreds and with the county justices. By the 1620s the Gloucestershire gentry were making determined efforts to wrest the inshire from the city, which the corporation struggled hard to resist.

Thus the charter of 1483 was something of a civic can of worms. It granted a number of important political privileges and liberties to the rulers and citizens of Gloucester; but by the end of the 16th century certain provisions in the charter were causing serious problems to the community, in some measure helping to poison the town's economic and political future.

First of all let us look at how the city was governed under the 1483 charter. Political and economic privileges were mostly restricted to the freemen or burgesses. Only burgesses could — officially — open shop and trade in the market; serve as or elect town officials and members of Parliament. But the freemen comprised no more than a minority of adult townspeople. In the early 16th century about 23 men a year were admitted to the freedom; by the mid-17th century the annual figure was about 35. At any one time the total number of burgesses was probably no greater than 500. As far as we know, none of the burgesses were women. One could obtain the freedom, either by birth (being the son of a freeman), or by serving as an apprentice to a freeman, or by paying an increasingly heavy freedom fine. All these ways tended to discriminate against the poorer classes and limit the freedom more to respectable craftsmen, merchants and traders.

In the early 16th century freemen were still admitted as burgesses of the ancient Gild Merchant. By 1600, however, this had finally disappeared and membership of the craft gilds and companies was more important. In 1634 there were 14 companies, including the mercers, tailors, bakers, tanners, innkeepers and butchers. Gilds regulated the activities of their own members and sought to prevent outsiders setting up in business in town. Evidence for most of Gloucester's gilds is patchy, however, and it is unlikely that they ever played the leading role in the ceremonial and political life of the town, that we find such organizations performing in other provincial centres (at York and Chester, for instance, the gilds staged plendid cycles of mystery plays in the 16th century). By the early Stuart period a number of Gloucester's craft companies were in decline and even where they prospered their functions were strictly regulated by the common council and magistracy.

The common council was chosen by co-option from the more substantial freeman and gild masters.[3] The customary number after 1483 was 40, but the figure fluctuated, depending on whether the aldermen were included in the membership. In addition, in 1605 James I reduced the number of the council to 30, though the total was later restored to the original 40. The common council elected certain town officers such as the four stewards or chamberlains, the town clerk and recorder. It also awarded leases of town lands, regulated the commons, levied taxes, and made ordinances for the general welfare and good order of the community.

By the late 16th century onwards, however, the council was overshadowed by the mayor and aldermanic bench. Aldermen were chosen by co-option from the more senior and wealthy ordinary councillors. By the last years of Elizabeth's reign they were principally recruited from the leading distributive traders and shopkeepers — mercers, grocers, and drapers — rather than from textile, tanning or other crafts. New aldermen were usually in their late 40s when they joined the bench and most were among the top tax payers in the city. The mercer Thomas Machen who became an alderman in 1574 and served as mayor three times in 1579, 1588 and 1601, was said to be worth £5-6,000 in land, sheep, money and personal goods and was accounted as 'rich or richer as any alderman or other alderman within the whole city.' He was lord of the manor of Condicote and owned or leased lands at Great Witcombe, Badgeworth and Eynsham. Most aldermen were probably somewhat less wealthy, though substantial men nonetheless.

The 1483 charter provided that the mayor should be elected by the aldermen and 12 senior councillors. In 1605 the electoral college was limited to the aldermen alone, but the old procedure returned in 1627. Constitutional changes of this sort were not terribly significant, however. In general the aldermen all took their turn at executing the office, a number like Thomas Machen holding the mayoralty several times.

In the century and a half after Richard III's charter the aldermanic bench steadily consolidated its control over city government. It tried increasingly to determine the outcome of municipal and parliamentary elections. From the 1590s members of the bench met together once or more times a week at the Tolsey, where they dealt with pressing administrative matters, particularly those concerning the poor. According to the 1483 charter the aldermen were *ex officio* justices of the peace, and by Elizabeth's reign they were exploiting the growing statutory powers entrusted to JPs to amplify and extend their authority. After 1605 the Gloucester bench presided over its own quarter sessions, which heard cases from both the city and inshire. Time again during the early Stuart period the aldermanic elite called the tune in civic administration.

How do we explain the growing power of this narrow magisterial caucus? Crown policy was undoubtedly influential. Whatever their dynastic disagreements, Richard III's Tudor successors shared his concern to strengthen the position of Gloucester's civic rulers. Under Elizabeth the Privy Council intervened repeatedly to back up the decisions and orders of the aldermen, mainly at the expense of the ordinary councillors. In 1605 James I's charter significantly weakened the position of ordinary councillors, though their rights were mostly restored in 1627. In town administration as well as in the counties the Crown preferred to deal with small groups of people that it knew, men who were loyal and who could be relied upon to defend royal interests in the locality.

But Crown interference was not the only cause of the growth of urban oligarchy. With the expansion of town populations in the 16th century, many leading inhabitants regarded some kind of restricted civic rule as essential to maintain effective public order. Gloucester's magistrates observed in 1584 how 'experience has taught us what a difficult thing it has always been to deal in any matter where the multitude of burgesses have voice.' Rule by a small group of town magnates also reflected the polarisation of wealth in the urban community. Already in the 1520s the parliamentary subsidy returns reveal that over 40 per cent of Gloucester's inhabitants who were taxed paid at the lowest rate, and only 6 per cent of those paying were assessed at the highest rates. Economic polarisation may well have become more acute during the following decades. On the one hand the population was swollen by an influx of lower class outsiders, many of them unskilled or semi-skilled migrants from the countryside; on the other hand some of the established industries, notably cloth-making and capping, went into terminal decline. In 1583 we hear that 'the trade of cappers and clothiers is utterly now so much decayed within the said city that whereas before Sir Thomas Bell and one Mr. Falkoner kept great numbers of people at work on spinning and knitting of caps, that now there are very few set to work in that trade and . . . there is the like decay of clothing.' Though other sectors of the urban economy did better, the number of wealthy people able and willing to perform the highest civic offices possibly diminished.

One sign of the problem was the growing incidence of townsmen who failed to attend civic elections or who refused to accept elevation to office. Even for those who were reasonably affluent the prospect of joining the bench was increasingly daunting. In the first place the central government and Parliament were imposing more and more duties and responsibilities on local officials — from setting-up workhouses and plague prevention to regulating apprentices and closing down alehouses. Again the high tide of poor people and vagrants flooding into the city, together with the mounting numbers of local unemployed and near destitute, bred multiplying problems of social control. In 1586 for instance there was extensive rioting in and about the city over grain shipments at a time of dearth. With only a primitive bureaucratic machinery to assist the magistracy, high civic office was a time-consuming business involving regular supervision of administration. It was also a costly exercise. For Gloucester, like many other corporate towns, faced growing financial difficulties in the 16th century. There is no time here to discuss the reasons for rising civic insolvency, but it is significant to say that by the 1570s there were large annual deficits and the city chamber had to be bailed out by members of the corporation. The four incoming stewards or chamberlains were required to lend the city enough money to clear the current deficit and were themselves reimbursed by the next set of stewards. However, in 1579 and again in 1584 and 1598 one or more of the new stewards refused to oblige and the financial system was threatened with bankruptcy. In 1584 the Privy Council had to intervene to compel the obdurate steward to make the necessary loan. Less spectacular, members of the aldermanic bench frequently dipped into their pockets to pay the lesser expenses of daily administration. Little wonder then that Gloucester's rulers came to be recruited from a small, self-perpetuating circle of urban magnates; men who also usually enjoyed the confidence and favour of the Crown.

The growth of civic oligarchy generated many problems, however. As we might expect those town leaders who spent long hours on official business, questioning perhaps vagrants from the North and other poor people suspected of petty crimes, or checking over the confusing figures of the chamberlains' accounts, activities which kept them away from their shop or trade, wanted some form of recompense. Likewise magistrates who lent to the town needed some return on their money. They demanded (and got) preferential leases of town or charity lands for themselves or their clients. They sold minor posts in town administration, together with alehouse licenses; they appropriated to their own use the city plate; they took bribes from inhabitants wanting favours such as exemptions from parish or military duties; they insisted on excessive fees for sealing documents; they managed to secure under-assessment (by their official colleagues) in the parliamentary taxation lists. In 1596-7 several aldermen were engaged in the fraudulent management of the municipal corn stock which had been established to supply the city's poor with subsidised grain; one of the offenders was alleged to have made a personal profit of £140-160 (this was at a time when the labourer's wage was between 40 and 50d a week). During the great plague outbreak of 1604 the mayor Thomas Rich was said to have sold the corporation over-priced shrouds and winding sheets for the poor.

Abuses were endemic in local administration in the early modern period. Indeed one might say they were a structural feature of civic government. But the scale of corruption at Gloucester towards the end of the 16th century went beyond generally accepted bounds of official behaviour. Combined with the expansion of aldermanic power and influence at the expense of the common council and freemen, it led to mounting tension and conflict. In 1586-7 there was a dispute over the election of a new recorder with a successful attempt by the outgoing man, Richard Pates, to nominate his successor William Oldsworth (who may have bought the office from Pates). In the parliamentary elections of 1588 the two more populist candidates, Thomas Atkins and Luke Garnons, were elected by the freemen. Political factionalism was recurrent during the late 1590s. At the parliamentary elections in 1597 it was alleged that the bench had deliberately excluded from the poll numerous freemen who were supporters of Atkins. Atkins in his campaign had appealed to the grievances of both ordinary townsmen and the inhabitants of the inshire, who felt themselves neglected by the city fathers.

The next eight years witnessed a spate of disputes and law-suits involving members of the ruling elite. Political instability was aggravated by the growth of conflict within the oligarchic circle. An establishment group led by alderman Thomas Machen and his son-in-law Thomas Rich, a group which was sympathetic towards Puritan ideas, was opposed by a party led by aldermen Garnons and John Jones, which endeavoured to mobilize the freemen vote and had closer ties with the cathedral close (Jones was registrar under eight bishops). When Rich became mayor in 1603 it was said that he spent 'the greatest part of his time and study that year to be revenged upon his enemies and such as were not of his faction, to weaken, charge and defame them'. There were further complaints that he held meetings of the council when he 'knew divers of the council of the city to be forth of the city and would only call some of his faction to counsel with him'. The elections to parliament in December 1603 were particularly turbulent. Rich and his allies on the corporation tried to delay the execution of the election writ, in order to prevent the return of John Jones. In the meantime Jones canvassed freemen support, promising to get more fairs for the city and offering satisfaction on other popular issues if he were elected. When Jones was eventually chosen Rich attempted to hold another poll to get the vote reversed — though without success. In the summer of 1604 Rich himself came under fierce attack. The city sheriffs asserted that Rich as mayor owed them £65, money which the sheriffs had to pay into the Exchequer as part of the feefarm to the Crown. While Rich was busy presiding over a meeting of aldermen to nominate officers for the next civic year, the sheriffs and their men marched on Rich's shop and carted away pieces of silk and velvet to cover the debt. In 1605 and 1606 much of this rather grubby political washing was exposed to public view in London when a series of cases was heard in Star Chamber. It must have been a chastening experience, for while further disputes occurred in 1608 and the mid-1610s, they were on a minor scale.

During the second half of James I's reign there are signs indeed that city government was settling down after the earlier uproars. There is little evidence of disputes in municipal or parliamentary elections. So far as one can judge, the bench was now firmly in the saddle. The aldermen consolidated their control through improvements in town administration and through their power as justices of the peace. Political divisions within the elite diminished, as the Puritan group came to predominate. A city lectureship had been established in St Michael's in 1598, with William Groves as the first preacher. In 1611 the new lecturer was the avowed Puritan Thomas Prior, and his successor in 1620 was John Workman, a strong critic of superstitious practices in the church. By the 1630s Gloucester had three or four weekly lectureships, the sermons supplementing ordinary parish services. At the same time, magistrates supported a godly reformation of manners, with a powerful emphasis on the sanctity of the Sabbath, an active campaign against drunkenness and alehouses, and increased control over city hospitals and the poor.

From the 1590s Puritanism won a growing following among better-off citizens who were influenced by trading contacts with godly towns like Bristol, Barnstaple and London. Merchants, traders and substantial craftsmen were increasingly literate and able to read the Bible and religious pamphlets and tracts. The godly surgeon John Deighton had a large collection of books in Charles I's reign, including John Foxe's book of martyrs and works by Calvin, Knox, John Bale, Stubbes and other Puritan writers. Alderman Singleton, according to John Aubrey, had 'the whole description of the funeral' of Sir Philip Sidney — one of the heroes of Elizabeth's war against Catholic Spain; this mobile was 'engraved and printed on papers pasted together' which stretched the length of a room and was 'turned upon two pins that turning one of them made the figures march all in order'.[4] Puritanism before the Civil War always had an important international dimension. But it had a vital communal role as well. For Gloucester's godly magistrates it helped provide a new coherence in civic politics. As well as helping to unite the ruling elite, it tended to buttress their authority and encouraged a sense of communal solidarity among the citizenry.

When Puritanism fell into disfavour under Charles I and preachers like John Workman were prosecuted by Archbishop Laud in the 1630s, Gloucester's magistrates rallied to the godly cause. They gave Workman a pension after he had been deprived by the High Commission; they fought hard to maintain their Puritan reforms; they may have supported emigration to New England. When Charles I's government began to crumble after the rebellion in Scotland Gloucester's leaders were advocates of reform in both Church and State. Thomas Pury, one of the city's MPs in the Long Parliament, was a leading exponent of the Root and Branch Bill. William Lenthall, Gloucester's recorder, was Speaker of the House of Commons when hostilities began with the king. Gloucester was a staunch supporter of Parliament throughout the Civil War. Even under the intense pressure of the prolonged siege during the summer of 1643, when Gloucester was bombarded by a large royalist army, the ruling elite held together remarkably well; there were relatively few defections to the king.

All this reflected in part the dominant power of the aldermanic caucus, its position increasingly strengthened and buttressed, as we have seen, in the decades since 1483. It also reflected the cohesive force of religious ideology. But another factor was no less influential. Civic unity and solidarity was made imperative by the growing threat from county landowners who in the years before and during the English Revolution showed themselves openly hostile to city privileges and determined to breach them.

The focus of gentry anger was Richard III's grant of the inshire hundreds to the city in 1483. If there were disputes between the city and county in the early Tudor period little is known about them. The first serious trouble occurred in the mid-16th century. Under Edward VI there seems to have been a controversy over musters in the inshire and according to a later report Mary's reign saw an action against the city to make it surrender the two hundreds. However, relations between city and county deteriorated markedly during the last part of Elizabeth's reign. In 1588 the magistrates refused to allow the Lord Lieutenant, Lord Chandos, to muster troops there. In 1595 there were clashes over shipments of malt by Gloucester men during the dearth, and over the levying of troops in the city and inshire for the war in Ireland. At midsummer quarter sessions a conference was arranged in the city between the county justices and town magistrates to resolve the differences, but when Gloucester's town clerk went to the New Inn, where the justices were sitting, to tell them the mayor and aldermen were ready to meet them, the county grandees said they were too busy. The mayor and aldermen waited at the Tolsey until 6 p.m. expecting a summons to attend, only to discover that by then the Gloucestershire justices had left town.

Positions polarised. Under James I Sir William Cooke of Highnam complained bitterly that the Gloucester magistrates profess 'hating to have a gentleman in any fellowship of government with them', and were refusing to grant leases of town land to local gentry. On the other side, the Guises of Elmore, important landowners in the inshire, sneered at the city declaring that though Richard III had granted the townsmen the inshire and they had large civic estates and a good port, 'they have neglected those advantages, depending too much on their powers on the incounty and levying moneys unduly, which although too little to enrich them is as yet enough to make them odious.'

There were three principal grievances raised against the city over the inshire. Firstly, as we have just noted, the burden of taxes and other levies was disproportionately weighted against the inshire. There may be some truth in this complaint, though it has to be remembered that the inshire area with its rich farmlands and Severn trade was probably much more prosperous than the city with its declining industries. Secondly, there was the charge that the gentry and inhabitants of the inshire had no say in the government of the city and so in their own administration. Finally, there was anger over the way that prosperous inshire men were deprived of a vote in parliamentary elections for Gloucester — unless they were freemen. More crucial, however, than these specific grievances was the growing political confidence and assertiveness of the county gentry, not just in Gloucestershire but in most parts of the kingdom. Increasingly prosperous, well-educated and socially self-conscious they were determined to demontrate their leadership of provincial society. Up and down the country town liberties suffered vigorous assault by local gentry.[5] Gloucester's jurisdiction over the inshire was a grave affront to the new-found political superiority of the Gloucestershire gentry and they were resolved to sweep it away.

In 1624 Sir William Guise held meetings of leading inhabitants of the inshire and denounced the mayor and aldermen 'with want of good education, with ignorance, partiality, malice, wrong justice, oppression and with unlawful' taxes.[6] Parliament was petitioned to let the inshire have its own MPs. And Guise and several other gentry obtained a special commission of association from the Crown which gave them authority to sit as justices of the peace. At midsummer sessions 1624, the Gloucester magistrates complained, the new JPs did 'unlawfully and turbulently enter into the said court of sessions and then and there hinder and interrupt the proceedings'. The city authorities at once counter-attacked. They protested that the gentry action threatened 'a settled and constant government' which had continued for 140 years, 'whereby an ill example will be given for knights and gentlemen to infringe and invade the liberties of all the cities of England.' Several hundred pounds was spent on legal suits and on lobbying Parliament and leading courtiers. By offering concessions which they later withdrew the city magistrates out-manoeuvred the landowners and the new charter of 1627 confirmed the civic powers over the inshire established by Richard III.

It was only a reprieve however, There were further clashes with the county in the 1630s. In 1638 the county (perhaps understandably) dragged its feet over donating money to relieve town victims of the plague epidemic. The city complained about breaches of the 1627 charter. When war broke out in 1642 and Gloucester sided with Parliament, some of the local gentry supported the king in retaliation and sent troops to besiege the embattled community. Gloucester's successful resistance against the royalists in 1643 gained it powerful parliamentary backing against its enemies, but by the early 1650s the landed gentry were once more on the offensive. By the late 1650s they were petitioning Parliament again, calling for the return of the inshire to the county. Gloucester played the anti-royalist card for the last time, avowing that the city had contracted the envy of persons disaffected to Parliament by our own 'constant adherence and fidelity to the same in the late wars.' No less serious, wealthy landowners refused to patronise city shops and traders and so further depressed the urban economy.

As long as the Parliamentary regime stayed in power, Gloucester's Puritan oligarchy could be fairly confident of retaining its own domination of city government and its jurisdiction over the two contested hundreds. But with the restoration of Charles II in May 1660 the tables were dramatically turned. Though the city conduits might flow with celebratory wine and the corporation present loyal addresses to the new king, the future for civic leaders who had defied the king's father in 1643 was bleak.

During 1660 and 1661 a number of leading Parliamentarians slipped away from Gloucester for the greater security of London. In 1662 when the Commissioners under the Corporation Act, mostly royalist gentry, visited the city they ejected more than three-quarters of the bench and common council. The same year the Marquess of Worcester supervised the demolition of those city walls which had so thwarted Charles I, while the great doors of the city gates were taken down and sent off to royalist Worcester. Worse still, a bill was introduced into Parliament providing for the severing of the inshire from the city. The magistrates petitioned against the measure, offering belated concessions to the gentry; but it was too late and in May 1662 the statute was passed and Richard III's troublesome grant was finally revoked.

It must have seemed like a total disaster. But it was not. The loss of the inshire ended a running sore in relations between the city and county, which now steadily improved. Under the new charter of 1672 a number of leading gentry joined the corporation. Gentry travelled to town in growing numbers to shop, consult lawyers and physicians, visit inns and coffee houses, take up residence in the cathedral precincts or nearby, politick and socialize. They brought growing business to Gloucester and the city, like many other county towns, came to bask in the lucrative warmth of gentry patronage.

The Restoration certainly caused a shake-up in the civic magistracy. It became less localised, more closely linked with provincial society and the wider world. This is not to say, however, that the decades after 1660 saw any major reversal in the growth of civic oligarchy. Oligarchic rule, first confirmed by Richard III's charter, remained the corner-stone of city administration until the Municipal Corporations Act of 1835.

Richard III's charter, then, for all its conferral of major privileges, never proved quite the civic success story that the inhabitants of Gloucester may have expected that late summer of 1483. The impetus which the charter gave to the growth of oligarchy, and the concessions of the inshire caused severe headaches for successive generations of city fathers. But for Richard at least it hardly mattered. Despite all his political manoeuvring he had been slain at Bosworth Field barely two years after the grant of the charter.

NOTES

For a more detailed account of the city's economic and political history in the 16th and 17th centuries see my contribution to the *Victoria County History* of Gloucestershire, Vol.4 (the City of Gloucester), forthcoming; also P. Clark, '"The Ramoth-Gilead of the Good": Urban Change and Political Radicalism at Gloucester 1540-1640', in P. Clark *et al.*(eds.), *The English Commonwealth, 1547-1640* (Leicester, 1979), pp.167-187; and P. Clark, 'The Civic Leaders of Gloucester, 1580-1800', in P. Clark (ed.), *Innovation and Tradition in English Provincial Towns 1600-1800* (forthcoming, 1984). My research on Gloucester has been generously supported over several years by the Social Science Research Council.

1. L. T. Smith (ed.), *The Itinerary of John Leland Parts IV and V*, (London, 1908), p.67.
2. P. Abrams and E. A. Wrigley (eds.), *Towns in Societies* (Cambridge, 1978), ch.7.
3. The common council books which provide the main record of corporation organization and activity during this period are in Gloucestershire Record Office, GBR B2/1, B3/1, B3/2.

4. A. Clark (ed.), *Aubrey's Brief Lives:II* (Oxford, 1898), p.249.
5. P. Clark and P. Slack (eds.), *Crisis and Order in English Towns 1500-1700* (1972), pp.24–5.
6. Disputes over the inshire from the 1620s onwards are recorded in Glos. Record Office, GBR B8/12.